HOW *to* MAKE HARD SELTZER

REFRESHING RECIPES *for* SPARKLING LIBATIONS

BY CHRIS COLBY

BREWERS PUBLICATIONS®

Brewers Publications®
A Division of the Brewers Association
PO Box 1679, Boulder, Colorado 80306-1679
BrewersAssociation.org
BrewersPublications.com

© Copyright 2020 by Brewers Association

All rights reserved. No portion of this book may be reproduced in any form without
written permission of the publisher. Neither the authors, editors, nor the publisher
assume any responsibility for the use or misuse of information contained in this book.

Proudly Printed in the United States of America.
10 9 8 7 6 5 4 3 2 1
ISBN-13: 978-1-938469-65-7
ISBN-10: 1-938469-65-8
Ebook ISBN-13: 978-1-938469-66-4

Library of Congress Control Number: 2020941048

Library of Congress Cataloging-in-Publication Data is on file with the Library of
Congress.
The following is for reference only:

Name: Colby, Chris
Title: How to Make Hard Seltzer: Refreshing Recipes for Sparkling Libations
Identifiers: ISBN: 978-1-938469-65-7; EISBN: 978-1-938469-66-4
Subjects: seltzer; cocktails; homebrew; low-carb; sparkling; craft-brewed

Publisher: Kristi Switzer
Technical Editor: David Wilson, Kris Kalav, Richard "Dee" Moore
Copyediting: Iain Cox
Indexing: Doug Easton
Art Direction and Production: Jason Smith
Interior and Cover Design: Danny Harms
Cover Photo: Luke Trautwein

*To scientists everywhere
who have fought to bring
light to the darkness.*

TABLE OF CONTENTS

FOREWORD

I STARTED HOMEBREWING IN THE MID-2000s when I was in my 20s. I fell in love with the creativity and the community that came with it. My first home-brew was a 100% extract wheat ale from a Mr. Beer® kit. Within six months I was brewing with grain and adding all kinds of crazy ingredients to my reci-pes. Fifteen years later, I sit as one of the cofounders and chief brand officer of Denizens Brewing Co., and I am also on the board of directors for both the Brewers Association and the Brewers Association of Maryland. Producing 3,000 barrels a year, Denizens is a small, craft brewery. I have been selling craft beer for over six years now and have a pretty good impression of what consumers are drinking. Guess what? Everyone who drinks alcohol—and I mean everyone—drinks hard seltzer.

Hard seltzer is one of the more lighthearted and fun drinks to enter the alcohol beverage space in a long time. Some of the most ardent craft beer fans love hard seltzer, myself included. People who love ESBs love hard seltzer. People who love fruited sours love hard seltzer. People who love oatmeal stouts love hard seltzer. People who love IPAs (hazy or otherwise) love hard seltzer. People who hate *beer* love hard seltzer. I could go on, but you get the point.

I have always believed that the more people who engage with the craft beer industry the better it will become. That includes drinkers and brewers alike. Why would we not jump on the opportunity to make and sell hard seltzer and potentially bring in new fans of our products? Who knows, maybe a new hard seltzer customer will like it so much that they will try one of our beers and enjoy that too? Craft brewers making hard seltzer is a win-win for everyone. We can bring so many more people to the craft brewing world by making this delicious beverage. Consumers can continue to support locally made products while enjoying imbibing a drink with lower calories, if that befits their lifestyle. And craft brewers do not have to concede the hard seltzer consumer market to multinational conglomerates.

At Denizens, adding hard seltzer to our core lineup has not detracted from our beers but has, in fact, complimented them. Just because we are making hard seltzers popular with drinkers does not mean we have to stop making great beer. We want all customers to feel welcome, and part of our mission is to offer flavors for every drinker. Everyone has a seat at our table, including hard seltzer fans.

If you are a brewery owner you should be paying attention to the rise of hard seltzers. After all, you are running a business and you want to make sure that you are making the products that consumers want to drink. And if you are brewing at home, why not add a new challenge? I know the thing that I love most about homebrewing is learning new recipes and challenging myself to make new styles.

The numbers tell a story. Hard seltzer is a skyrocketing category in the alcohol beverage space. In fact, according to Nielsen[1], hard seltzer's highest grossing week ever was the week leading up to July 4th, 2020. Generally speaking, consumer trends are showing that sales of low-calorie and gluten-free options are growing. Being a low-calorie, light, and easy-drinking product, hard seltzer is the number one choice of drinkers who are carb conscious.

Adding hard seltzer to your lineup is not only a short-term play, but in the long term it will ensure your brewery's success. We should all be making the products that our customers want to buy if we want to survive. For those of you who are still skeptical about adding hard seltzer to your product list, here is the good news: there are still people who want to drink beer. I am not arguing that we should stop making beer. I am arguing that our industry should not miss out on a vast group of folks who would drink our products if we simply added hard seltzer to our lineups.

---

[1]   Justin Kendall, "Nielsen: Hard Seltzers Post Strongest Sales Week Ever During July 4 Holiday Period," Brewbound, July 13, 2020, https://www.brewbound.com/news/nielsen-hard-seltzers-post-strongest-sales-week-ever-during-july-4-holiday-period.

If you picked up this book then you are at least curious about hard seltzers and thinking they are something you may want to try and make. Hard seltzer is a simple drink, but very easy to mess up when brewing it. I wish this book existed when we started making seltzer two years ago. Our team at Denizens spent a year honing recipes, production processes, yeast choice, carbonation levels, and flavor profiles before releasing our first version. You will find in the following pages an enormous amount of information to help you get started and perfect your recipes. The author, Chris Colby, is a long-term and avid homebrewer, has a formal education in biology and chemistry, and has been writing about beer and brewing for 20 years. You should listen to him.

I will say it again: hard seltzer is the fastest growing category in the alcohol beverage space, period. It has been experiencing double-digit growth for years now and there are no signs of it slowing down. And yet, until now, there have been no books or training materials on how to actually make it. That is what this book is for. You are about to read the only book solely dedicated to crafting hard seltzer. Not only will you find recipes and discussions of production processes, raw materials, and ingredients, but also a rundown of the regulations involved in classifying and labeling this new product. If you are a homebrewer, this book also includes recipes and brewing process tips aimed specifically at you.

I am looking forward to trying all the delicious versions of hard seltzer you all come up with. I cannot wait to toast one with you!

Julie Verratti
Co-Founder/Chief Brand Officer, Denizens Brewing Co.

ACKNOWLEDGMENTS

I'D LIKE TO THANK EVERYONE involved in this project, including all the brewers who took time out of their busy schedules to talk to me about their processes. I'd like to thank everyone who worked with the manuscript, including the reviewers Dee Moore (Pretoria Farms Cooperative), David Wilson (Alaskan Brewing Company), and Kris Kalav (ATPGroup); and the copyeditor, Iain Cox. I'd also like to thank Kristi Switzer (Brewers Association) for giving me the opportunity to write this book—and my upcoming book on science and brewing. And finally, I'd like to thank my wife for putting up with me.

INTRODUCTION

T HIS IS AN EXTREMELY TROUBLED time for craft brewers. Prior to 2020, many breweries were struggling to keep up with craft beer drinkers' demand for new beers. In the "good ol' days," before the craft beer revolution, brand loyalty was very strong among beer drinkers. Budweiser drinkers drank Budweiser, period. They would turn their noses up at other brands, even though they might not have been able to pick them out in a triangle test. Not so among craft beer drinkers in 2019, who always wanted the newest thing—invariably another variation on IPA. Meanwhile, sales of classic craft beer brands suffered at the hands of an ever-changing lineup of hazy, "juicy" IPAs. One potentially bright spot for brewers, at least from a sales perspective, was the rise of hard seltzer. From 2016 through 2019 sales of hard seltzer kept rising and many breweries were hopping on the bandwagon to brew these (usually) unhopped brews. Hard seltzers were, surprisingly, selling to all age groups and, perhaps more surprisingly, selling to both men and women equally.

Then came the COVID-19 pandemic. In most US states brewpubs closed, able only to serve curbside to-go orders, and watched as beer in their brite tanks slowly went stale. Production breweries had it a little better with grocery store sales not directly affected, but some liquor stores were only selling beer by curbside pickup. At time of writing, with the pandemic ongoing, numerous brewpubs and craft breweries are on the brink of going out of business.

So, this is a book on hard seltzers. If you are a professional brewer it is possible you are reading this out of necessity and not a love of hard seltzers. Brewing hard seltzers may allow you to keep your brewery afloat during the COVID-19 crisis. And, when the dust settles on the pandemic, it may bring greater profits to your brewery. In this book, I outline the steps required to brew a hard seltzer and give example recipes for production breweries and brewpubs. You will, of course, most likely formulate your own recipes, but the recipes here will give you a starting point, something to build on. I also review the federal regulations for brewing these "beers."

Although hard seltzer might not excite anyone in your brewery, except for your sales manager, it is an interesting beverage for technical reasons. Brewing a good hard seltzer is a challenge for any brewer. There is a trick to getting brewer's yeast (or wine yeast or distiller's yeast) to ferment a solution of just sugar. Ending up with a crystal-clear, neutral base, with the aroma and flavor of alcohol being the only organoleptic characters detectable, likewise takes some skill. The best advice I can give—which I repeat multiple times throughout the book—is to test everything. Taste test your water. Taste test your recipe ideas using clear hard seltzer and your chosen flavoring and acid. And definitely test to determine the level of yeast nutrients required to allow your chosen yeast strain to ferment your neutral base.

The history of the beverage is also somewhat interesting. Although hard seltzers are wildly popular now, nobody was asking for them before they were introduced. A change in Alcohol and Tobacco Tax and Trade Bureau (TTB) regulations allowed sugar to be substituted for malt and some brewers rolled the dice.

If you are a homebrewer, you are probably reading this book out of curiosity. Maybe someone in your household likes hard seltzers and you thought you would give it try. Or perhaps you enjoy technical challenges and thought you could expand your brewing horizons. Well, here is some good news—despite what some may say, you absolutely can brew a decent hard seltzer at home. I give the full procedure for how to brew hard seltzer at home and a handful of recipes covering the most popular types of hard seltzer. (The flavors are all interchangeable.) For the homebrewer, running the fermentation is the most difficult aspect of making a hard seltzer. However, if you brew your hard seltzers at working strength this aspect is not insurmountable. Producing a hard seltzer this way allows you to run an ordered fermentation that yields a neutral base requiring little cleanup. (And hey, you're a homebrewer—it's OK if your hard seltzer isn't perfectly clear, but you can certainly make it respectable.)

Brewing a strong neutral base and diluting it to working strength is something that advanced homebrewers may want to tackle for the sheer challenge, but it takes a substantial effort to clean up the strong neutral base after fermentation.

Both professional brewers and homebrewers will, of course, likely experiment and push the boundaries of hard seltzers. (Imperial barrel-aged hazy hard seltzer anyone? Anyone? . . . Hello?) For its part, this book will at least help you identify where the current boundaries are.

If you are not a brewer, you can at least gain an appreciation of the effort that goes into making a hard seltzer. And as a bonus, the final chapter is on mixing cocktails based on hard seltzers. Anyone can try these, even if they are not a brewer.

I hope you enjoy the book. Now that I am done writing it, I need a beer.

© Getty/dkidpix

1

HISTORY

H UMANS HAVE BEEN BREWING FOR many thousands of years. The history of brewing is expansive, endlessly fascinating, and well beyond the scope of this book. Still, hard seltzers are mostly brewed beverages, so a little brewing history can help us think about their place in the world of fermented beverages. In this chapter I will review some of the highlights of brewing history, paying attention to the ingredients, the brewers, and the drinkers. Where it is known, I will also point out to what extent societal customs and government regulations have affected the course of brewing. All of these things are relevant to the continued rise of hard seltzers today.

SPRINGTIME FOR BREWING

Archaeologists have found evidence indicating that the earliest known brewing occurred in three distinct regions: ancient Mesopotamia, which encompasses modern-day Iraq, southwest Iran, Kuwait, northeastern Syria, and southeast Turkey; ancient Egypt; and ancient China. These archaeological findings date back to at least 5,000 BC. The earliest brews did not resemble modern, commercially produced beers, of course. In addition to grain (including barley or spelt), some of the earliest beers incorporated fruits or spices. None were hopped, the first recorded use of hops in beer not appearing until the ninth century.

The earliest beers were not carbonated, as there were no pressure vessels to hold them. Neither were they crystal-clear—even if they had been, there were no clear glass vessels to view them through. Ancient pictures depicting drinking in Mesopotamia show a group of people drinking a beverage, described in texts as "cloudy and thick," through straws. Both the Egyptians and the Mesopotamians brewed multiple types of beer, and beer was available to all regardless of social status.

The earliest brewers had to malt their own grain, relying on whatever grains were grown in the region. Likewise, if their beers were spiced, brewers were limited by whatever spices grew locally or were available through trading. The same went for honey and fruit, ingredients also present in early beer. Archaeologists have identified writings about beer—such as the Hymn to Ninkasi—and analyzed residues in pottery from ancient sites that, together, describe a wide variety of ingredients appearing in beers from various times in various cultures.

Another shared aspect of many ancient beers is that they were likely brewed by women. Archaeologists believe that much ancient brewing was done by priestesses in service of their religion.

SUMMERTIME FOR BREWING

From its earliest beginnings, brewing spread to almost every culture and beer was brewed wherever grains were grown. Throughout the Middle Ages in Europe—lasting from the fifth through the fifteenth century—brewing was done mostly by individual families or farms. In Scandinavia, for example, each year farms were required to produce enough beer for their residents. As in ancient times, brewing was predominantly the business of women. The term *alewife* refers to such women. Although brewing was mostly a household or farmstead practice, monastic brewing started in the fifth century. The fermentable carbohydrates in most beers came from malted grains, which included barley, wheat, oats, and others. Beers were often spiced with a wide variety of bittering agents.

In many places, there were restrictions on brewers. For example, in thirteenth-century England, all ale production was regulated by the Assize of Bread and Ale. (An *assize* was originally a county court held periodically to administer civil and criminal law; gradually, the word also came to mean a statute for the regulation of weights and measures and the price of commodities.) The Assize of Bread and Ale tied the price of ale to the price of grain and specified that ale had to meet certain quality standards to be sold publicly. After reaching Europe's shores in the mid-fourteenth century, the Black Death (bubonic plague) is estimated to have killed 75–200 million people in Eurasia from 1347 to 1351. After the Plague subsided there was a rise in wages due to a labor shortage. For a variety of reasons, there was also a rise in the standard of living, cheaper grain, and a movement toward larger ale houses and brewing became more modernized. As brewing transitioned from being something done mostly by individuals to larger, commercial enterprises, men became the primary brewers of beer. By the 1700s in Europe, guilds had formed to license brewers and brewing became industrialized. This pushed lone women brewers and small female brewing enterprises further to the side.

Through most of the nineteenth century, brewers in the Western tradition recognized English, German, and Belgian brewing practices and tastes as being the most influential in the modern world. In the twenty-first century the United States, a Johnny-come-lately in terms of history, is now exerting its own considerable influence on the brewing world.

ENGLAND

Throughout the mid-twentieth century, the English brewing scene was heavily influenced by English pub culture. Most neighborhoods had a pub and regulars would gather to drink milds and bitters, often with drinkers in a group taking turns buying a round. These beers were low in alcohol by today's standards, often around 4%, and this was partly because the taxes on more highly alcoholic beers made them more expensive. High-alcohol beers such as barleywines and old ales existed, but were not the everyday drink of most working-class Englishmen. It is unlikely that beer drinkers clamored for low-alcohol brews. Instead, English pub culture evolved around the low-ABV ales that resulted, in part, from high tax rates on stronger beers.

GERMANY

In Germany, fears that too much wheat was being used for brewing led to the *Reinheitsgebot* of 1516, often referred to as the German Beer Purity Law. This law restricted the ingredients in beer to water, barley, and hops. Brewers at the time did not have a full understanding of the role of yeast in brewing and so it is not mentioned. The full text of the *Reinheitsgebot* is:

> We hereby proclaim and decree, by Authority of our Province, that henceforth in the Duchy of Bavaria, in the country as well as in the cities and marketplaces, the following rules apply to the sale of beer:
>
> From Michaelmas to Georgi, the price for one Mass [1,069 mL] or one Kopf [slightly less than one Mass], is not to exceed one Pfennig Munich value, and
>
> From Georgi to Michaelmas, the Mass shall not be sold for more than two Pfennig of the same value, the Kopf not more than three Heller [a Heller is usually one-half Pfennig].
>
> If this not be adhered to, the punishment stated below shall be administered.
>
> Should any person brew, or otherwise have, other beer than March beer, it is not to be sold any higher than one Pfennig per Mass.
>
> Furthermore, we wish to emphasize that in future in all cities, market towns and in the country, the only ingredients used for the brewing of beer must be Barley, Hops and Water. Whosoever knowingly disregards or transgresses upon this ordinance, shall be punished by the Court authorities' confiscating such barrels of beer, without fail.
>
> Should, however, an innkeeper in the country, city or market-towns buy two or three pails of beer [containing 60 Mass] and sell it again to the common peasantry, he alone shall be permitted to charge one Heller more for the Mass or the Kopf, than mentioned above. Furthermore, should there arise a scarcity and subsequent price increase of the barley (also considering that the times of harvest differ, due to location), We, the Bavarian Duchy, shall have the right to order curtailments for the good of all concerned.

Although touted as a law that ensured "beer purity," it was partly enacted to prevent brewers from competing with bakers for the available wheat and rye on the market. While it is true that brewing with barley does indeed produce great beer, there is no evidence that beer drinkers at the time the Reinheitsgebot appeared preferred all-barley beers to those brewed with other grains. If that had been the case, there would have been no reason to order brewers to use only barley. As in Britain, German beer drinking culture adapted to the constraints imposed by the government.

BELGIUM

Belgium's beer culture is idiosyncratic in a lot of ways. And its history is no exception. Arguably, Britain and Germany's beer cultures were shaped by government constraints that resulted in a lineup of beers that would not have been brewed in the absence of those constraints. British brewers would probably have made at least slightly stronger beer for sale if it was more affordable to do so, something consumers would most likely have embraced. Likewise, German brewers and beer drinkers would likely have enjoyed producing a wider variety of beers if never roped in by the *Reinheitsgebot*. In the case of Belgian brewers, however, legislation actually opened the door for brewers to flourish and perhaps to appeal more to consumer preferences.

In 1919, the Vandervelde Act prohibited the sale of spirits at pubs. The legislation was named after Emile Vandervelde, Belgium's Minister of Justice and a vocal teetotaler. It allowed for the sale of spirits, which included jenever, a distilled beverage that was a favorite in Belgium, only at liquor stores. However, the minimum purchase was two liters and spirits were taxed heavily. The law was supposedly aimed at preventing public drunkenness by the working classes, hence the ban on selling spirits in pubs and the prohibitive cost for anyone wishing to buy spirits to drink at home. However, the Vandervelde Act placed no prohibitions on beer. In the years since then, excepting during the Second World War, the Belgian beer industry flourished, producing a dizzyingly wide variety of interesting, and oftentimes unique, beers. The Vandervelde Act is sometimes credited with spawning the boom in Belgian high-alcohol beers, but some beer historians dispute this, pointing out that most of the well-known examples of highly-alcoholic Belgian beers appeared only fairly recently in the 1980s. On the other hand, Duvel—the 8.5% strong golden beer brewed from Pilsner malt and sucrose—was introduced soon after the Vandervelde Act. What can be said is that the constraints on purchasing spirits did slow their sale and brewers stepped in to fill the void with a vast selection of beers.

What all of this illustrates is that, in many cases, the beers available in a country at any given time do not exist simply due to what brewers want to brew and consumers want to buy. Taxes, proscribed ingredients, and other constraints play a role in every country's beer culture. Other variables not discussed here—most notably technological advances—also drive changes in brewing.

WINTER ARRIVES

Zima was not the first "malternative" beverage (or alcopop), but it was the first to gain, and for a reasonable period, keep, a national distribution and the attention of consumers. This clear, lemon-lime flavored beverage was introduced in 1993 by the Coors Brewing Company under the name Zima Clearmalt. (Just a year earlier, Crystal Pepsi had been introduced to the soft drink market.) The word *zima* means "winter" in the Slavic languages. Brewed using some malt, and at 4.7%–5.4% ABV, Zima was pitched as an alternative to beer. A year after its introduction, Coors estimated that 70% of US beer drinkers had tried it.

Zima was derided both in beer circles and the popular media. Late-night TV talk show host David Letterman repeatedly referred to the beverage as a "girly-man" drink and the product never shook the reputation of being aimed at women. (Early on, this accusation was also leveled at hard seltzers, but sales of hard seltzers indicate they are equally popular with men and women.) This image was hard to shake, and Coors told retailers not to stock Zima next to the sweeter, and definitely women-associated, wine coolers. In 1995, Coors tried to woo male drinkers with Zima Gold, a beverage that was golden in color and featured a faint hint of bourbon, but it tanked within the year. Coors also tried to do to Zima what Miller Brewing Company did to its Miller Lite beer—masculinize it by tying it to sports. Advertisements featuring young men enjoying a Zima after an apparent pickup game of football failed to do what Bubba Smith, Dick Butkus, Larry Csonka, Bob Uecker, and others succeeded at doing for Miller Lite.

Coors sold 1.3 million barrels of Zima in 1994, but sales dropped to 403,000 barrels in 1996. Despite this, Coors kept it in production for another 12 years. Sales rebounded a little when the company increased the lemon-lime flavoring and began advertising the drink for its thirst-quenching properties. Nevertheless, Zima went out of production in the US in 2008, although it had a limited re-release in 2017. It is still produced in Japan.

Other clear beers followed, including Miller's Clear Beer, Pabst's Izen Klar, and Stroh's Clash, but none gained any traction. On the other hand, alcopops such as Smirnoff Ice and Bacardi Breezer did succeed in carving out a niche for themselves.

After Zima, a variety of flavored malt beverages came and went. A few, such as Mike's Hard Lemonade, were briefly a hit. Originally introduced in Canada in 1996 as a cooler with spirits added, Mike's Hard Lemonade was reformulated as a flavored malt beverage for the US market. The Mark Anthony Group, who later introduced White Claw hard seltzers, was the company behind it. The reformulated, malt-based version of Mike's Hard Lemonade was launched in Boston on April Fools' Day in 1999. It quickly gained ground and began boasting strong sales despite competing malt beverages from both Anheuser-Busch and Miller. In fact, in 2016, Mike's was one of the fastest-growing beer brands in the US. (When reporting on sales figures, all brewed beverages are grouped under "beer," which includes flavored malt beverages.) Between 2009 and 2016 the company doubled in size and the number of products expanded to 14, including higher-alcohol versions.

Later, in 2015, one of the best-selling craft beers in the US was Not Your Father's Root Beer. There has been some discussion of how this beverage, which some call a hard soda but falls into a craft beer data set, is made. The brewery (Small Town Brewery) claims that it is a traditionally brewed beer flavored with spices typically found in soft root beers. However, some within the industry have speculated that it is a flavored malt beverage, citing its sweetness. Still others, citing Small Town's higher-alcohol version of the drink (10.7% ABV), claim that it must be spiked with neutral grain spirits. In addition, there is evidence that the brewery is not a small, independent brewery but instead is connected to Phusion Projects, the makers of Four Loko. However Not Your Father's Root Beer is made, this flavored alcoholic beverage preceded hard seltzers and is yet another example of something marketed either as a beer or a substitute for beer that tastes different from any traditional beer.

In 2016, the Mark Anthony Group released White Claw. This drink was made possible by a change in TTB regulations allowing sugar to be used as a substitute for malt in beers. The company believed that millennials would be receptive to a drink that was low in calories,[1] low in carbohydrates, and gluten-free. White Claw seltzer had approximately the same alcoholic content as beer but gave a vague impression of being healthy. Sales grew each year, and many other breweries began brewing their own versions. At first, hard seltzers were selling most strongly in the warmer months, but around 2019 they began showing strong sales year-round. Whereas most flavored beers, malternative beverages, and alcopops in the past became stuck with a reputation of being

---

1   Throughout this text, *calorie* refers to the large calorie (Calorie, or kilocalorie) used to express the energy content of foods.

only for women, hard seltzers appealed equally to both men and women. And, although targeted at younger drinkers, older drinkers began enjoying them too. Dismissed by many as likely to be a fad when they were introduced, most beverage industry analysts believe hard seltzers will continue to gain market share in the next few years.

CREATING CONSUMER APPEAL

Long story short, lots of different forces have shaped brewing throughout its history: availability of ingredients, improved technology, and government intervention (often in the form of taxes). These variables have had both positive and negative influences, but one thing absent from this discussion is consumer desire. Many of the changes did not come about because consumers desired something. This is also the case with hard seltzers. In 2015, there was no consumer outcry for clear, alcoholic, fizzy beverages with a light fruit flavor. A change in US government regulation via the TTB allowed brewers to make hard seltzers that would be taxed at the rate of beer (or malt beverages). Consumer demand followed the trend, it did not precede it.

Hard seltzers racked up over $1 billion US sales in 2019. Ever since their introduction, many people have dismissed them as a fad. Usually, these dismissals were not based on evidence and showed a lack of understanding about the nature of the appeal of the beverage. A December 2019 article in Forbes opined that hard seltzer is not likely to be a fad, citing the fact that 30% of consumers who bought a hard seltzer made a repeat purchase. Also in late 2019, financial services company UBS predicted hard seltzers would reach $2.5 billion in annual sales by 2021. As signs continue to point to growth in this segment, more and more breweries are jumping on the bandwagon. In early 2020, Anheuser-Busch introduced its line of Bud Light Hard Seltzers. Industry experts claim the company has invested $100 million to get in on this market.

Hard seltzers are marketed toward younger drinkers. They have been labeled a "social media beverage" given the influence social media has had on their sales. Comedian Trevor Wallace contributed to awareness of hard seltzer when he released a June 2019 video in which he claimed, "Ain't no laws when you're drinkin' the claws, baby," a reference to White Claw. The video had over 3,700,000 views by late 2019.

Rightly or wrongly, many drinkers believe drinking hard seltzers is "healthier." The drinks are low in carbohydrates and calories, which is widely believed to explain their appeal. In 2019 Twitter traffic, "low carb," "low calorie," and "keto" are three terms strongly associated with the beverage. ("Keto" here refers to a ketogenic diet, a high-fat, low-carbohydrate diet originally formulated to help treat children with epilepsy, but which has recently become a fad diet for people wishing to lose weight.) On social media sites, drinkers are most likely to post pictures of themselves drinking hard seltzer in social situations. Discussions of the beverage itself are generally limited to it being low in calories and low in carbs—and, of course, that it contains alcohol. There is virtually no discussion of the flavor, aroma, or any other characteristic of the beverage itself. These characteristics that typify hard seltzers—calorie content, carbohydrates, alcohol, flavors—are outlined further in chapter 2.

Although initially viewed as drink for millennials, hard seltzer is making inroads with older drinkers as well. Perhaps more importantly, despite early indications that the drink was perceived as "feminine," hard seltzer is appealing to male and female drinkers equally. By contrast, beer's popularity is highly skewed toward men, whereas wine's popularity is higher with women.

In 2018, sales of hard seltzer rose in the early part of the year and were especially strong in the period between Memorial Day and Labor Day, after which they declined. In 2019, sales of hard seltzer continued to rise throughout the year, ending speculation that hard seltzer might become just a seasonal, warm-weather beverage.

Hard seltzer detractors tend to be drinkers who focus on the organoleptic properties of the drink. How can people continue to buy something that "tastes like TV static" they ask? The answer is that this is not what people are buying into—they are buying a beverage that is the thing that young, trendy, pseudo-health-conscious people are drinking. Rising sales, the fact that both men and women are buying them, and a drop in seasonality all hint that hard seltzers are here to stay.

© Souders Studio

2

HARD SELTZER CHARACTERISTICS

ALTHOUGH OTHER MALTERNATIVE BEVERAGES HAVE at least a 30-year history, depending on your definition of malt beverage, drinks called hard seltzers only began rising to prominence in 2016. This was the year White Claw was introduced. Since then, the number of hard seltzer brands has grown continually. Some of these beverages are labeled spiked seltzers, spiked spritzers, sparkling hard seltzers, or some other combination of these terms. A few of these actually are spiked, in the sense that they have a distilled spirit added to a base seltzer. However, for tax purposes, most are brewed beverages. The market has already started to produce variations on the basic hard seltzer theme, but the most popular hard seltzers have several things in common—and a few things that separate them from beer and other malternative beverages.

CALORIES AND CARBS

A basic hard seltzer is a low in calories compared to many other alcoholic beverages. The most popular brands have 90–100 calories per 12 fl. oz. serving. In contrast, the same size serving of typical American light Pilsner beer ranges from 95 to 110 calories, with ultra-low-calorie beers such as Miller Genuine Draft 64 and Bud Select 55 having 64 and 55 calories, respectively. Most regular American Pilsners weigh in at 140–150 calories. India pale ale (IPA), which is currently the most popular craft beer type, typically contains between 180 and 230 calories.

In addition to their low caloric content, many hard seltzer brands tout the low amount of sugar or carbohydrates in their beverages (typically 2 g per 12 fl. oz. serving or less) as a selling point. The sugar and caloric content of hard seltzer is much lower than that of previous incarnations of malternative beverages. From table 2.1, it can be seen that today's hard seltzer contains roughly 100 calories and 20 g of carbs less than the previous generation of malternative beverages.

Table 2.1 Caloric and carbohydrate content of beverage brands per 12 fl. oz. serving

Brand	Calories (kcal)	Carbohydrates (g)
Zima	181	21
Smirnoff Ice	228	32
Mike's Hard Lemonade	220	33
Not Your Father's Root Beer	177	12

Together, the low calorie count and low sugar or carbohydrate content is meant to appeal to "health-conscious drinkers" (which may sound a bit oxymoronic), especially those on diets that restrict carbohydrate intake, such as ketogenic diets, the Atkins diet, Whole30, and the South Beach diet. Many brands additionally label themselves as gluten-free, something that distinguishes them from beer, even though, ironically, some are categorized as beers by the TTB rather than as malt beverages.

ALCOHOL CONTENT

Typical hard seltzers contain 4%–5% alcohol by volume (ABV), are highly carbonated, dry to semi-sweet, and lightly flavored. "They taste like a La Croix [a brand of flavored seltzer water] with a shot of vodka added," says Ashton Lewis, brewmaster at Springfield Brewing Co.

FLAVORS

Hard seltzers come in a wide variety of flavors, as well as unflavored. In late 2019, I surveyed 24 hard seltzer makers, including all of the best-selling brands, and found 45 different flavors represented. The flavors mostly came from fruits, including citrus fruits, stone fruits (drupes), and berries (aggregate fruits).

Grapefruit and lime are the most popular citrus flavors found in hard seltzers. Cherry and mango are the most popular stone fruits. And raspberry, strawberries, and blackberries are all popular aggregate fruits. Other flavorings include vegetables (cucumber), herbs (basil and rosemary), and flowers (hibiscus and elderflower). A small number of hard seltzers include "rosé" in their name, which could indicate a color only or a color and flavor associated with any red fruit.

Some hard seltzers are flavored with a single fruit or other flavor. Others have a combination of flavors. Single-flavored seltzers and seltzers with a flavor combination exist in roughly equal numbers in the examples I surveyed. From the top 24 producers, I found 53 seltzers with a single flavor listed, 52 with two flavors listed, and one with three flavors listed. Additionally, I found multi-flavored hard seltzers sold as mixed berry, piña colada, and mojito, for which the actual number of different flavors in each is unspecified. The top two seltzer producers, White Claw and Truly, favored single flavors to flavor combinations (at a 15:2 ratio), indicating that single flavors may be more popular in terms of volume produced.

SINGLE-FLAVORED SELTZERS

The single-flavored seltzers available in the ones surveyed range from simple, "crowd-pleasing" flavors (e.g., cherry and lime) to slightly more sophisticated, or at least less common, flavors such as prickly pear and dragon fruit. The most popular flavor is grapefruit, alternately listed as grapefruit, ruby grapefruit, or ruby red grapefruit. Thirteen of the top 24 brands produced a grapefruit-only seltzer. Cherry, in all but one case listed as black cherry, was the second most popular flavor, with seven instances. The top three seltzer producers—White Claw, Truly, and Bon & Viv—all offer grapefruit and black cherry single-flavored options, so these flavors assuredly lead in both numbers of brands produced and overall volume of that flavor brewed. Lime and pineapple were the next most

© Getty/Roman Samokhin

abundant, each with six examples. Out of the top three producers, only White Claw offered a lime-only flavor. However, lime was also the flavor most likely to be part of a combination of flavors, and Truly and Bon & Viv offer a raspberry lime and a lemon lime seltzer, respectively. The next most popular single flavors are mango (4 instances); cranberry and watermelon (each 3 instances); and orange, lemon, passion fruit, and peach (each 2 instances).

FLAVOR COMBINATIONS

Roughly half of hard seltzer offerings examined come with a combination of two flavors. In some cases, these combinations are seemingly intended to appeal to slightly more sophisticated palates than the average single-flavored beverage. One manufacturer, Press, even advertises that it uses "foodie" flavor combinations (Press's hard seltzers also contain more sugar and calories than is typical). Although plenty of hard seltzers feature two flavors, there are only two flavor combinations that appear more than once—these are lemon lime and raspberry lime, each produced by two different brands. Lime was the flavor most likely to be one-half of a flavor combination, with nine instances of lime being paired with another flavor. Lemon was the second most popular flavor found in flavor combinations. Raspberry, strawberry, and blackberry all had four instances (so did rosé, which again could indicate either a color or an unspecified flavor and its corresponding color.) There were three instances of flavor combinations that include blueberry, cherry, cucumber, lemonade, or peach; this includes blueberry acai, cherry lime, cucumber peach, blueberry lemonade, and mango peach. If herbs or flowers are a listed ingredient, they are always paired with a fruit; examples include watermelon mint, melon basil, black cherry and rosemary, blackberry hibiscus, and lemon elderflower. The only example of a seltzer with three flavors listed is lemon agave hibiscus offered by Wild Basin Boozy Spiked Seltzers, a brand of Oskar Blues.

The numbers cited here are just a snapshot in time and will certainly change. The overall pattern—simple single-flavored products in roughly equal numbers with slightly more elegant two-flavor combinations—is unlikely to dramatically change. Also, when I write about simple flavors and slightly more sophisticated flavors, the word "slightly" is important. It is unlikely that anyone with a refined palate would view any of the hard seltzer flavors as complex or compelling. These are simple, inoffensive beverages that can be drank (quickly, if desired) without

© Getty/Photozek07

requiring any contemplation. The simplicity of these beverages is another of the possible reasons for their sudden success, beyond appealing to health-conscious drinkers. If you are standing at the seltzer display in a store, trying to decide between hard cherry and lime, it is unlikely that anyone is going to tell you his opinion of a particular brand, the brewery that makes it, the ingredients they use, or whether its maker is independent or owned by a larger company. These are simple beverages aimed at consumers who want to make simple choices regarding their belch-fueling tipsy water.

Table 2.2 Common hard seltzer flavors commercially available in descending order of abundance

Flavor	Comment
Grapefruit	Sometimes as Red Grapefruit or Ruby Red Grapefruit
Lime	Singly and as one half of a flavor combination
Lemon	Singly, paired with other flavors, or as lemonade
Cherry	Almost always Black Cherry
Pineapple	
Mango	
Cranberry	
Watermelon	
Orange	
Peach	
Passion fruit	
Raspberry	Often with lime
Strawberry	Usually paired with another flavor
Blackberry	Usually paired with another flavor
Acai	Paired with blueberry
Cucumber	Paired with peach
Mint	Paired with watermelon
Basil	Paired with melon
Rosemary	Paired with blackberry and hibiscus
Hibiscus	Usually paired with another flavor
Elderflower	Paired with lemon

Notes: Order of abundance as of June 2020. Unflavored hard seltzers are also fairly popular.

CARBONATION

Like plain seltzers, much of the appeal of hard seltzers is their spritz. Hard seltzers are typically carbonated to around 2.8 volumes of CO_2, slightly higher than a typical craft beer or American Pilsner (which are usually around 2.4–2.6 volumes of CO_2). There is no lasting foam in a hard seltzer, but its fizz tickles the tongue and wafts the beverage's (typically faint) aroma up to the drinker's nose. Brewpubs that make hard seltzers often push them at the same CO_2 pressure as their beers. This results in a lower level of carbonation but avoids potential problems with excessive foaming in the draught system.

Table 2.3 Typical carbonation levels in fermented drinks

Beverage	Volumes of CO_2
British pub-style ale	2.2
European lagers	2.4–2.5
Typical American craft ale	2.5
American-style Pilsner	2.5–2.6
Soda pop (cola, etc.)	3.5–5.0
Belgian-style tripel	4.0
German hefeweizen	4.0–5.0
Soft seltzer	3.0–5.0
Champagne or sparkling wine	6.0

Notes: Figures given are for the most typical examples of the beverage. Higher and lower levels can be found.

CALORIES: ALCOHOL AND SWEETNESS

Hard seltzers are lightly flavored and not overtly sweet, being far less sweet than soft drinks (e.g., Coca-Cola, Dr. Pepper, and Mtn Dew). Many hard seltzer producers list the amount of calories per 12 fl. oz. serving on their packaging, with most being in the 90–100 calorie range. This is lower than most soft drinks, which typically contain 140–160 calories in the same size serving. However, the 90–100 calories in hard seltzer comes mostly from its alcohol. In a soft drink all of the calories come from sugar, most often high-fructose corn syrup.

Pure ethanol has 1,905 calories per 12 fl. oz. serving. Thus, the alcohol in a drink that is 4.0% ABV would have 76 calories; a 5.0% ABV drink would have 95 calories. Given the known caloric content of most hard seltzers, this leaves little room for sweetness from sugars. A 4% ABV seltzer with 90 calories from alcohol would have 14 calories from carbohydrates. This leaves room for 3.6 g of sugar per 12 fl. oz., assuming there is no other source of calories. Similarly, a 5% ABV seltzer with 100 calories from alcohol will have 5 calories remaining from carbs—meaning just 1.3 g of sugar per 12 fl. oz. In contrast, a 160-calorie soda has 43 g of sugar per 12 fl. oz. serving. The amount of sugar with which you can potentially back sweeten a hard seltzer is further reduced if there are any residual carbohydrates left after fermentation. (Back sweetening refers to adding sugar to a beverage after fermentation, then preventing fermentation of that sugar. This sweetens the beverage.) In total, this means back sweetening will be limited to 0.50–1.3 oz. (14–37 g) sugar per US gallon (3.8 L) or, equivalently, 15–42 oz. (0.43–1.2 kg) per US barrel (31 US gallons, or 117 L). This is not much. In contrast, back sweetening a bone-dry wine to 2% sugar—putting it at the low end of semi-sweet wines—would take about twice as much sugar, around 2.7 oz. (77 g) per US gallon or 84 oz. (2.4 kg) per US barrel.

As with the sweetness, the intensity of the flavor additions in hard seltzer is low. The typical amount of flavoring added is around 0.7–3.0 mL/L. This is equivalent to 2.8–12 fl. oz. (86–355 mL) per US barrel.

The sweetness of fruits in their native state varies. So does the level of acidity and the type of acid found in the actual fruit. In some cases, the fruit flavoring in a seltzer may not be as appealing as the flavor of the actual fresh fruit because there is less sweetness associated with it. In other words, the fruit flavoring may not contain sugar. In a similar manner, the fruit flavor added to a seltzer may be improved if the seltzer's acidity is brought closer to the level of acidity of the native fruit.

For this reason, you might think that seltzer producers would stick to flavors derived from low-sugar fruits. In this way, the flavor of the fruit would be tasted with a similar level of background sweetness that consumers would expect from the native fruit. But although lime and cranberry (two low-sugar fruits) are popular flavors, so too are cherry and mango. These latter two fruits have a relatively high sugar content in their natural state, but the cherry and mango flavors used in hard seltzers do not necessarily contain sugar.

Table 2.4 Typical alcoholic strength
of various fermented beverages

Beverage	Alcohol by volume (ABV)
Hard seltzer	4%–5%
American pale ale	5%–5.5%
American-style Pilsner	5%
American-style IPA	6%–7%
British pub bitter	3.5%
Foreign export stout	6%–8%
German Oktoberfest	6%
German bockbier	6%–7%
German hefeweizen	5%
Strong Belgian ale	6%–12%
White wine	9%–11%
Red wine	11%–16%
Sweet mead	8%–12%

Notes: Values are given for most typical examples. Weaker and stronger versions of any of these beverages are not hard to find. Consult the BJCP Guidelines for the accepted ABV ranges of beer styles recognized in homebrew contests.

ACIDITY

Hard seltzers are not sour, but most have a level of acidity that gives the beverage some "zing" that complements the fruit flavor. Some of the acidity comes from carbonic acid, a weak acid that forms naturally when carbon dioxide is dissolved in water. However, additional acids are frequently also present in a hard seltzer.

As a fruit ripens its acidity drops as its sugar level rises. At harvest most fruits are sweet but still have enough acidity to make them tangy. Raspberries and Granny Smith apples, for example, both have a prominent tart edge to them. The acidity in these two fruits is the result of different acids. The most abundant acid in raspberries is citric acid; the most abundant acid in Granny Smith apples is malic acid. When making a fruit flavored hard seltzer, the brewer should accentuate the acidity, if needed, with the appropriate acid for the fruit.

Citric acid is the most abundant acid in strawberries, raspberries, and many other berries. It is also, as the name implies, the most abundant acid in citrus fruits. Lime, grapefruit, lemon, and orange are all popular citrus flavors in hard seltzers. And citric acid is frequently seen on the ingredient list of beverages with these flavors.

Malic acid is the most abundant acid in cherries, blueberries, peaches, apricots, pears and plums. It is also abundant in apples and especially prominent in sour apples. Green apple candies, for example are sometimes flavored only with malic acid. The name "malic" comes from the Latin *malus*, meaning apple (the genus of the domesticated apple is *Malus*).

Tartaric acid is an acid best known as a component of grapes. The potassium salt of tartaric acid, potassium bitartrate, crystallizes and often forms "wine diamonds" when grape juice is fermented. Grape is a popular flavor in non-alcoholic beverages. However, at the time I surveyed available hard seltzer brands there were none with grape flavoring. This is likely due to potential problems related to grapes being the most common fruit from which wine is made. Wine is taxed at a different rate than beer. So, even though up to 49% of the ingredients in a beer can be grapes and it still be classified as a beer, many brewers shy away from putting out grape beers. (The recent rise of rosé beer is an exception to this pattern.)

Other acids play a key role in the flavor of some fruits. In some cases, the appropriate acid may be a part of the flavoring mix. In other cases, it may be added separately. None of the popular hard seltzers are overtly sour, but most have a level of acidity that, along with the level of carbonation, gives them a refreshing quality.

Table 2.5 Most abundant acids found in various fruits used as flavorings in hard seltzers

Citric acid	Lime, lemon, grapefruit, orange , pineapple, blueberry
Malic acid	Apple, pear, banana, raspberry, cherry, apricot, peach, watermelon
Tartaric acid	Grape, tamarind
Quinic acid	Cranberry

In general, citrus fruits (e.g., lime and orange) contain a high amount of citric acid. Drupes (e.g., cherry and peach) usually contain a lot of malic acid. Most common berries (e.g., raspberry and strawberry) have substantial levels of both citric acid and malic acid, with malic acid usually being more abundant. Individual cultivars may vary.

VARIATIONS

Already, there are many variations on the hard seltzer theme. Perhaps the most expected are the higher-alcohol versions. Pabst Brewing Company was one of the first to offer a hard seltzer with more kick, releasing an 8% ABV hard seltzer. The Anheuser-Busch Natural Light brand was another early entrant in the higher alcohol derby with their 6% ABV lineup of boozy seltzers. There are a variety of others now.

Other companies have introduced sweeter examples. Press, for example, with their 110-calorie offerings, gives drinkers a sweeter, but higher-calorie, option. White Claw went the other way, at least temporarily, with a lineup of 70-calorie, 3.7% ABV seltzers. There are also brands, such as Crook and Marker, who use artificial sweeteners like stevia to improve the flavor of their offerings without increasing the calorie count.

Some breweries are also coming up with new variants that are not a result of simply tweaking the existing variables. Alaskan Brewing Company is using local ingredients in their lineup, namely sitka spruce. Also, multiple breweries in states where it is legal have offered CBD-infused or THC-infused hard seltzers. (There are soft seltzers infused with these compounds as well.)

Since their introduction in 2016, hard seltzers have been characterized as relatively low-calorie and low-carbohydrate beverages, typically supplying between 90 and 100 calories and containing less than 2 g of sugar per 12 fl. oz. serving. Most examples currently on the market are 4%–5% ABV. As they are marketed toward health-conscious drinkers, some brands also tout that they are gluten-free. Already, however, producers are making some hard seltzers with more or less sugar or more or less alcohol. Hard seltzers are typically lightly flavored and highly carbonated, with fruit flavors dominating the flavor choices. The light fruit flavor is often accentuated with a hint of acidity from citric or malic acid. In the next chapter, we will take a look at the ingredients that go into making hard seltzers.

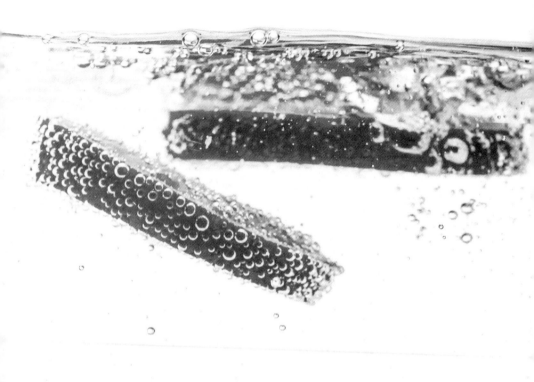

© Getty/heinstirred

3

INGREDIENTS

The INGREDIENTS IN A TYPICAL hard seltzer include water, sugar, and a flavoring. As we saw in chapter 2, the impression of the flavoring may be enhanced by the addition of the appropriate acid or by back sweetening.

Yeast ferments the initial sugar mixture and yeast nutrients are required to "feed" the yeast. The flavoring and other ingredients are added after fermentation. If the beverage is back sweetened, a stabilizing agent is required. This can either be potassium sorbate or heat pasteurization. Yeast and yeast nutrients may be thought of as either an ingredient or a processing aid; whatever category a brewer puts them in, their role in brewing does not change.

Although most hard seltzers are made from fermented sugar, some formulations include malted barley and hops. These beverages can be identified as a malt beverage under TTB regulations. Otherwise, the beverage will be categorized as a beer. (And yes, that is the opposite of how most brewers think of it.) If malted rice is included in the recipe, the brewer may be required to add enzymes to ensure complete conversion of the rice's starch. One of the most notable features of a hard seltzer is its fizziness. As such, it is reasonable to think of carbon dioxide as an ingredient. Indeed, the Food and Drug Administration (FDA) says it is and carbon dioxide, or carbonated water, has to be listed specifically.

WATER

Most hard seltzers are roughly 95%–96% water and none of the remaining components of a hard seltzer are strongly flavored. As such, it is important for brewers to ensure the quality of their water. The requirements for water used in brewing a hard seltzer are very similar to those for brewing liquor. It needs to be potable (of course), and free from any compounds that give it off-odors or flavors. Most municipal water sources will deliver suitable water in these respects. Some well water sources may contain iron, which makes them unsuitable for brewing.

DEALING WITH CHLORINE

Brewers using municipal water sources need to remove the chlorine compounds that have been added to the water to suppress microbial growth. The most commonly used primary disinfectant is chlorine, which is added to the water at the treatment plant. The most common secondary disinfectant in municipal waters is monochloramine, a.k.a. chloramine (NH_2Cl), which is synthesized by replacing one of the hydrogens in ammonia (NH_3) with chlorine. Monochloramine is added to the water as it leaves the treatment plant because monochloramine is more stable than chlorine, maintaining its disinfectant properties for longer in the distribution system. As a consequence, monochloramine is also harder to eliminate from water than chlorine. Chlorine will evaporate from water, given time; heating and agitation will increase the evaporation rate of chlorine. Unfortunately, evaporation does not work with monochloramine.

Most breweries deal with chloramines by filtering their water through activated charcoal. Some homebrewers neutralize chloramines by treating their water with sodium metabisulfite or potassium metabisulfite, the active ingredient in Campden tablets. One tablet treats 20 gallons (76 L) of water and the reaction occurs almost instantaneously. If any chlorine remains in the water, treatment for chloramines will remove it. Any established brewery will already be processing their water to remove these disinfectants, so no additional action beyond what is done to produce water suitable for brewing is required for brewers of hard seltzers.

Brewing liquor—the treated water used for brewing beer—additionally requires certain amounts of particular ions in order to set the proper conditions in the mash. The proper level of calcium ions is especially important. However, since the fermentable carbohydrates for most hard seltzers do not come from malted grains that have been mashed, the mineral requirements for beer do not apply to hard seltzers, excepting those that include a small amount of malt in their formulation.

If the hard seltzer does use malted grains, the usual recommendations for brewing liquor are that it contain 50–150 parts per million (ppm) calcium ions. Additionally, for pale beers, the usual recommendation is that the alkalinity of the water—expressed either as ppm or mg/L $CaCO_3$—not exceed 50 ppm. Alkalinity is a measure of how much acidity a solution can absorb. In brewing water sources, alkalinity is usually roughly equivalent to the concentration of bicarbonate ions (HCO_3^-). For darker beers, in contrast, the most advantageous levels of alkalinity may climb to around 200 ppm. For hard seltzers, below 50 ppm would be best.

The combination of calcium ions, magnesium ions, and bicarbonate ions in brewing liquor influences the pH of a beer's mash. The mash pH also sets the stage for the pH to drop lower in the boil and during fermentation. In a hard seltzer made from only sugar these pH changes do not occur. As such, if a brewery has a standard brewing liquor for making pale beers, using it would be the simplest approach.

YOUR LOCAL WATER SOURCE

Brewers who use municipal water sources have probably consulted their city's water analysis reports at some time. These will give the level of calcium, carbonate, and magnesium ions in their water, along with the standard measures of water purity. Keep in mind that these reports are generally either from a single point in time or an average over a longer period of time. Municipal water sources can change as cities switch between different wells or other (surface) water sources. If you are brewing hard seltzers, always taste test each batch after the chlorine compounds have been removed and assess its suitability. Beyond simply being potable, the water should also taste good.

If your brewery's water source has off characters, these should be remedied. In most cases, filtration through activated charcoal will be the best approach.

In the case of water with a very low amount of dissolved minerals, minerals such as calcium chloride or calcium sulfate may be added to improve the taste of the water. It should not take over 50 ppm of either calcium chloride or calcium sulfate to do that. However, bottled water sold as mineral water may have total dissolved solids in the 200–1,500 ppm range. So, feel free to experiment with levels of minerals up to this amount. Adding minerals should really only be necessary if you are using reverse osmosis (RO) water. Still, it is easy to quickly tell if adding a small amount of minerals affects the taste of your brewing water.

SUGAR

Table sugar (sucrose) is the most abundant, and in many cases the only, fermentable carbohydrate in most hard seltzers. In some cases, glucose—or even high-fructose corn syrup (HFCS)—can be used instead of sucrose. As very nearly 100% of the sugar will be fermented in a well-run fermentation, sucrose or glucose does not add sweetness to the drink; it is merely in the recipe to be consumed by yeast to produce alcohol and carbon dioxide. If sweetness is desired, the beverage can be back sweetened.

Sucrose is most commonly sold as granulated sugar, consisting of small white crystals, that is isolated from sugar cane or sugar beets. However, there are other forms of sucrose. Brown sugar is primarily sucrose with either a bit of molasses retained from the refining process or molasses added back to refined white sugar. Sucrose may also be sold as powdered sugar, or confectioner's sugar, which is sugar ground to a fine consistency. Powdered sugar often has up to 5% of an anti-caking agent added, usually corn starch or tricalcium phosphate. The molasses in brown sugar and anti-caking agents in powdered sugar make them unsuitable for hard seltzer production. Regular white granulated sugar is, obviously, the preferred choice

Sources of Sugar

Back in the 1400s, sugar was an expensive luxury. Now it is a relatively cheap commodity. If anything, some nutritional experts say it is too cheap. The low cost of sugar is another reason, outside of tax concerns, that brewing hard seltzers can be profitable. Most brewers know at least a little about the production of barley and hops, which are the two main

© Getty/pioneer111

agriculturally produced ingredients in beer. However, they may not be aware of how sugar—the second-most abundant ingredient (after water) in hard seltzers—is produced.

The two main sources of sucrose are sugarcane and sugar beet. Corn, or maize, is the primary source of glucose (dextrose) and also the source of high-fructose corn syrup. Here I give a brief overview of these three crops. The information here does not have any implications for how hard seltzer is produced in your brewery; it is simply (hopefully) interesting information that will allow you to take a wider view of the ingredients you use.

Sugarcane

Sugarcane is the largest food crop in the world in terms of harvest weight; corn (maize) is second and rice is third. Seventy-nine percent of the world's sugar comes from sugarcane, with the crop being worth US$24 billion in 2011. In 2016, 41% of sugarcane in the world was grown in Brazil. In the US, sugarcane is grown commercially in the Gulf states, from Texas to Florida. If you are a gardener in USDA hardiness zones 9–10, you should be able to grow sugarcane in your area.

Sugarcane is a grass species in the genus *Saccharum*, which is in the family Poaceae. Among the grasses, sugarcane is closely related to sorghum (*Sorghum*) and slightly more distantly related to maize (*Zea*). It is even more distantly related to the cereal grains, including rice (*Oryza*), wheat (*Triticum*), barley (*Hordeum*), oats (*Avena*), and rye (*Secale*). There are many species in the genus *Saccharum*, but most commercially grown sugarcane is *Saccharum officinarum*. *S. officinarum* is native to New Guinea but is now grown worldwide in most tropical and subtropical climates. Another species of sugarcane, *S. sinense*, originated in southeast Asia and was domesticated in what is now Taiwan and southern China.

Sugarcane is a tall perennial grass, with each plant's 3–4 stalks reaching 10–13 ft. (3–4 m) in height. Commercially, it is propagated clonally by planting cuttings. The time until maturity varies from 8 to 22 months, depending on where sugarcane is grown. The plant will die if it freezes during this period. Twelve to sixteen percent of the plant is soluble sugars found in the internodes of the plant. (The internode is the space between nodes, which are the locations that branches and leaves emerge from.) Sugarcane is grown so that these sugars can be extracted and, in

© Getty/fcafotodigital

many cases, refined for human use, either for direct consumption or for fermentation (and sometimes later distillation) to produce beverages and fuel. The unprocessed plant is also used as animal feed.

Sugarcane is grown mostly in regions that do not experience freezes. If freezing does occur, the sugarcane must be harvested before the first frost. If not, it is harvested when the plant reaches peak maturity. Rain will make the sugary mass in the internodes less concentrated, so sugarcane is not harvested during rainy periods.

During harvesting, the plant is cut just above ground level, leaving the roots and ideally 2.8–3.9 in. (7–10 cm) of each stalk undisturbed. This allows the plants to spring back from their roots and produce another crop, called a ratoon crop. A ratoon crop is a crop that grows from the "stubble" of a previous crop. Rice, sorghum, bananas, and pineapples are grown this way. Ratoon crops mature faster by at least a month than planted crops. The ability to ratoon is one of the most important characteristics of commercial sugarcane cultivars.

In the past, the cutting was largely done by manual laborers with machetes or similar cutting devices. Sometimes, the field was burned prior to harvesting. Today, except where labor is extraordinarily cheap, harvesting is done by machine. The harvester cuts the leaves from the top of the stalks and cuts the stalks into short lengths, called billets. Once the leaves in the field dry out, they are burned—returning nutrients to the ground but not allowing disease to propagate. After two or three ratoon crops have been harvested, the field should be plowed and a new crop, preferably legumes, rotated in.

Sugar Beet

Sugar from sugar beet (*Beta vulgaris* subsp. *vulgaris*) accounts for 20% of global sugar production. In the US, it accounts for 54% of domestically produced sugar according to the American Sugarbeet Growers Association (ASGA).
Despite this, sugar beet is not even in the top 30 crops globally by either harvest weight or economic importance. In 2013, the last year for which numbers were available, Russia, France, the United States, Germany, and Turkey were the top five producers. In 2017 in the US, sugar beet was grown in North Dakota, northern Minnesota (USDA hardiness zones 2 and 3), Michigan (zone 5), and other scattered locations (up to zone 8).

© Getty/luiscarlosjimenez

According to the ASGA, there were 23 factories to process the sugar from this crop. By 2011, 95% of sugar beets grown in the US were GMO (in this case, being Roundup Ready, i.e., immune to glyphosate herbicide.)

Sugar beet is a subspecies of the common beet (*Beta vulgaris*), which lies in the Amaranthaceae family, the same family as spinach, quinoa, and many ornamental plants. Commercially grown sugar beet belongs to the Altissima cultivar group. The wild ancestor of the sugar beet is the sea beet, *B. vulgaris* subsp. *maritima*. Swiss chard belongs to the same species as sugar beet but is a different cultivar. Other *B. vulgaris* subsp. *vulgaris* cultivars are beetroot (the common garden or vegetable beet), borscht (formerly called blood turnip), and mangelwurzel (grown for fodder).

Cultivated beets are biennial. In the US sugar beet is a temperate crop that is hardy to zone 8 and takes 100 days to reach maturity. It is subject to black root rot. Most sugar beet crops are wind pollinated, although some are insect pollinated. Commercially grown sugar beets are harvested mechanically and the fields rotated with maize or wheat every 4–6 years.

The weight of a single sugar beet is 1.1–2.2 lb. (0.5–1.0 kg) and contains 12%–21% sugar (the rest is roughly 75% water and 5% pulp). The ASGA claims that the root is 18% sucrose. The sugars in sugar beet are stored in the root, which can be colored red, white, or yellow. Refined beet sugar is the same as refined cane sugar.

Corn (Maize)

Corn (*Zea mays*), or maize, is the second largest crop worldwide by harvest weight. In 2012, roughly 885,000,000 metric tons of corn was harvested, compared to 1,800,000,000 metric tons of sugarcane. (Of course, this compares the weight of the corn cobs to the weight of the entire sugarcane stalk.) The US is largest corn producer, harvesting 371 million metric tons in 2017, worth about US$26 billion. China was second at 259 million metric tons, and Brazil came a distant third, with 98 million metric tons.

Corn has many uses. Aside from food for humans and animal feed, 40% of US corn production is used to produce ethanol to be used as a fuel additive. A substantial amount of corn is converted into corn syrup and high-fructose corn syrup, either of which can be used in hard seltzer production.

© Getty/Atoss

In the US, the top five corn-producing regions are centered on north central Iowa. These regions are northern Iowa, northern Illinois, central Nebraska, southern Minnesota, and western Indiana. However, corn can be grown almost anywhere in the US. (Sweet corn, a North American garden favorite, can be grown in USDA zones 3–8.) Successfully growing corn requires full sun, rich soil, and temperatures over 50°F (10°C) for most of the growing season.

Corn has shallow roots and as such is prone to lodging. Lodging is when the plant is blown over by the wind or knocked down by heavy rain. Corn borers are the most important insect pest while smut fungus is an important pathogen.

Zea is a genus of grass in the family Poaceae. It is relatively closely related to sorghum and sugarcane and more distantly related to cereal grains. Corn grows as vertical stalks, commonly 10 ft. (3 m) tall, but taller varieties exist that can grow up to 43 ft. (13 m). Fully-grown corn has 20 leaves. Each leaf extends from a node on the stalk, facing the opposite direction as the previous leaf. In rich soil, the central stalk may develop side branches called tillers (or suckers). When the plant reaches its full height, or nearly so, it develops a "tassel." The tassel is a branched structure at the top of the plant on which the male flowers develop. Later, the female flowers develop inside a presumptive corn cob. Corn is wind pollinated and pollen from the tassels floats onto the "silks" of corn ears. The silks are the pollen tubes that conduct pollen to the ovaries on the cob. Each ovary forms a corn kernel.

Corn is a facultative short-day plant and needs temperatures over 50°F (10°C) for most of its growing season. The development of hybrid corn raised yields from around 70 bushels per acre in the 1970s to around 220 bushels per acre today. GMO corn varieties are able to grow in cooler climates with less irrigation, and require less tilling because weed control is done by pesticides that the corn plant has been engineered to be resistant to. The reduction in tilling saves on fuel costs and decreases the amount of erosion caused by farming. About 85% of corn grown in the US is genetically modified, with Roundup Ready corn (i.e., resistant to the herbicide glyphosate) being the most popular type grown.

Maize was domesticated from the grass teosinte (*Zea mays*) in the Tehuacán valley of Mexico. Geneticists believe there was initially a single domestication event 9,000 years ago. The major differences between the wild teosinte ancestor (*Zea mays*) and modern corn (*Zea mays* subsp. *mays*) is mostly due to two genes, grassy tillers 1 (*gt1*) and teosinte branching 1 (*tb1*).

Sucrose is a disaccharide, composed of two monosaccharide sugar residues, glucose and fructose, joined together. Glucose and fructose are both 6-carbon sugars with the molecular formula $C_6H_{12}O_6$. Although their molecular formulas are identical, the arrangement of their atoms (their conformations) differ. Glucose can take the form of a linear molecule or a six-membered ring. Fructose can take the form of linear molecule or a five-membered ring. In sucrose, the glucose and fructose units are in their ring, or cyclic, conformation. The molecular formula for sucrose is $C_{12}H_{22}O_{11}$. You will notice this is not exactly equivalent to two monosaccharide molecules because a molecule of H_2O is released when the glucose and fructose bind together. For reference, maltose—the most abundant sugar formed when malted grains are mashed—is also a disaccharide. It is composed of two cyclic glucose residues linked together and has the same molecular formula as sucrose ($C_{12}H_{22}O_{11}$).

Brewer's yeast can use sucrose as a carbon source. The yeast takes in sucrose and breaks it into its component monosaccharides—glucose and fructose—via the enzyme invertase. When glucose and fructose are separately available to brewer's yeast, glucose is used preferentially. However, yeast raised in a fructose-only environment process fructose almost as quickly as yeast raised in a glucose-only environment process glucose. The presence of high levels of glucose also suppresses the utilization of maltose, if that is also present in the mix.

Glucose (also called dextrose) is available as crystals or as syrup. High-fructose corn syrup may also be used. Other sugar sources, including agave syrup and honey, can supplement the refined sugars in the formulation, but these are more expensive and any flavors or aromas contributed by additional sugar sources may be stripped by fining or filtration.

The sugar base fermented to make a hard seltzer is frequently more concentrated than the final product. As with high-gravity beer production, a higher-gravity solution is fermented and then diluted to working strength when it is packaged. The dilution must be done with de-aerated water to keep the product from staling prematurely. High-gravity brewing saves on tank space. However, the higher the gravity of the initial sugar mixture, the longer it will take to ferment, all other variables being equal. Also, high-gravity fermentations may be more susceptible to the off-aromas associated with stressed fermentations, not to mention the possibility of a fermentation that finishes prematurely. For this and other reasons detailed below, before dedicating a full-scale production tank to a sugar fermentation, I recommend at least one smaller scale test fermentation.

If you use brewer's yeast, a fermentation of a 15–22 degrees Brix (°Bx) sugar wash can be performed. The resulting 7.6%–11% ABV neutral base can then be diluted such that the final alcohol content is 4%–5% ABV after the addition of the flavoring. If you are using wine yeast or distiller's yeast, fermentations up to 30°Bx can be attempted. For smaller breweries, including brewpubs, fermenting the sugar solution at working strength may be the best approach, especially if generating the required volume of de-aerated water is difficult.

Using Degrees Brix

A value in degrees Brix (°Bx) defines the weight/weight (w/w) percent of sucrose in an aqueous solution. If 100 g of an aqueous solution contains 1 g of sucrose it is 1°Bx. The density of a sugar solution measured in degrees Brix is roughly equivalent to its density in degrees Plato (°P). The differences are small at lower concentrations, but the disparity increases at larger values. For example, 0.00°Bx is 0.00°P but 22.0°Bx is 22.9°P. Since the Brix scale is meant for measuring sucrose concentrations and the base of hard seltzers is fermented sucrose, I will use degrees Brix rather than degrees Plato, even though the latter is more familiar to brewers.

MALT

Some hard seltzers contain malted grains. This is usually so that the brewer can categorize the hard seltzer as a malt beverage rather than a beer. In order to qualify as a malt beverage to the TTB, a brewed beverage must contain 25% malted barley and 7.5 lb. of hops per 100 bbl. (29 g/hL). At the time of writing, this is under reconsideration by the TTB and the ruling may change.

Malted barley may be used, but any color and flavor from it will need to be removed by filtration or fining later. Malted rice is frequently used in hard seltzers as it is colorless and flavorless. Depending on the diastatic rating of the malted grain, exogenous enzymes may be needed to ensure complete conversion of the starches to sugars. This is not required for malted barley, but it may be for malted rice. Even when malted grain forms a low percentage of the total fermentables, the unconverted carbohydrates from a mash may need to be degraded further to make a sugar wash with a fermentability high enough for a hard seltzer.

For the purposes of keeping the color low, some of the malt in the grain bill may be chit malt. Chit malt is barely malted barley, with a color usually around 1.4 degrees Lovibond. This is lower than most Pilsner malts, even undermodified ones. Because it is very lightly kilned, chit malt has a very high diastatic power. Chit malt is comparatively high in protein, however, so it may lead to foam in the final beverage, something not normally seen in hard seltzers.

HOPS

Hard seltzers do not exhibit any hop bitterness. Still, if you want your hard seltzer to qualify as a malt beverage according to the TTB, you need a minimum of 7.5 lb. of hops per 100 bbl. (29 g/hL) of product. The first instinct for many brewers might be to use dried hop cones (or pellets) with the lowest alpha acid rating. However, there are other approaches. The TTB regulations do not specify unused hops. To satisfy their requirements, spent hops from a beer wort boil can be used. Spent hops are not only very low on residual alpha acids but carry some water weight that dried hops do not. Brewers using spent hops should rinse them thoroughly so that color from the beer does not carry over. Note also that the TTB requirements call for hops, not hop cones. Adding 7.5 lb. per 100 bbl. of hop leaves or stems—which do not contain lupulin glands, and hence have no alpha acids—would satisfy the requirements. Spent T-90 pellets are also available.

YEAST STRAINS AND YEAST NUTRIENTS

A wide variety of yeast strains may be used for fermenting hard seltzers. The best yeast strains should be fast fermenters, attenuative, and neutral. Yeast strains with comparatively low nutrient requirements are also a plus. Brewers will want their fermentations to quickly proceed to near or complete dryness and for the resulting fermented mix to be free of strong flavors or aromas. Different breweries use brewer's yeasts, wine yeasts, or distiller's yeast to ferment their hard seltzers. Among brewer's yeast strains, those used for neutral ale fermentations are the best.

In order to ferment a solution of sucrose (or glucose) and water, yeast nutrients are required. Sugar provides the carbon source for the fermentation but living yeast cells require other nutrients to be healthy. If yeast health is not considered, the fermentation will stall and never finish.

In some ways, wine fermentation is a lot like hard seltzer fermentation. This is one reason many producers use a wine yeast for the task. The fermentable sugars in wine are glucose and fructose from the wine grapes. However, the grapes contribute a small amount of other biological molecules (esp. proteins and amino acids) as well as trace amounts of some minerals. Still, for most commercial wine fermentations, a winemaker will add yeast nutrients to ensure a rapid, complete fermentation. Two of the biggest considerations when adding yeast nutrients are nitrogen and zinc.

The nutritional requirements of yeast strains vary, but in most cases yeast requires at least 300 ppm free amino nitrogen (FAN) to conduct a healthy fermentation. As the name implies, FAN is nitrogen that is available to yeast ("free" as opposed to bound) and this comes in the form of amino acids, compounds that contain nitrogen. Another measure of nitrogen available to the yeast is yeast assimilable nitrogen (YAN), which is the amount of FAN plus ammonia (NH_3) and ammonium (NH_4^+) in solution. Nitrogen that is a part of proteins—long chains of amino acids bound together—is not accessible by yeast because yeast does not break down proteins. An odd upside to all-sugar mixes having no other nutrients is that calculating the amount of yeast nutrients to add to reach your FAN target is simple. There is no need to test the original mixture to determine the existing level of FAN (or YAN), as is done in wine, because it is zero. If the yeast strain requires 425 ppm YAN to ferment properly, then all you need do is add 425 ppm of nitrogen via the appropriate yeast nutrient.

Diammonium phosphate (DAP) is a yeast nutrient that is widely used by winemakers to supply some of the nitrogen yeast requires. The formula for DAP is $(NH_4)_2HPO_4$, and in solution it supplies ammonium ions that the yeast can use. (DAP is also a fertilizer that farmers spread in their fields to give their plants nitrogen.) In wine fermentations, DAP is typically used at rates of 0.41–0.83 oz./bbl. (10–20 g/hL).

Excessive DAP levels can have negative effects and should be avoided. A fermentation in which the yeast has access to more nitrogen than it needs can be "overstimulated" and give off excess heat. This can become a positive feedback loop, stimulating more yeast activity, which heats up the fermentation more. In addition, excess nitrogen in the neutral base can become fuel for the growth of contaminating microorganisms. Some winemakers refer to DAP as "yeast crack"—yeast cannot get enough of it but it can quickly become bad for them if used in excess. Yeast nutrient blends often contain DAP, so be careful if you plan to use DAP along with a "complete yeast nutrient," as is common practice in winemaking.

Zinc is another required nutrient that is completely absent from sugar solutions. A concentration of 0.2 ppm zinc will keep most yeast strains healthy. You can add zinc sulphate heptahydrate, which is 25% zinc by weight, to supplement your other yeast nutrients, if required.

Blends of DAP and other compounds beneficial to yeast are often sold as complete yeast nutrient or yeast energizers. These usually contain an inorganic source of nitrogen (DAP), an organic source of nitrogen (amino acids from ground up yeast cells), zinc, and other compounds. The ground up yeast cells provide a wide spectrum of trace nutrients. Many types of blended yeast nutrients are available commercially and there is no need to develop your own blend unless you are using a yeast strain with unusual nutritional requirements. Some distiller's yeast strains are sold packaged with the appropriate yeast nutrients for them.

The manufacturers of yeast nutrients give a recommended range for their products. Generally yeast nutrients that contain a higher percentage of DAP are required in lower amounts. Addition rates vary from 0.12–0.60 oz. per bbl. (3.4–17 g per bbl.). Homebrew recommendations are generally ¼–½ tsp. per 5.0 gal. (19 L) for yeast nutrients that do not contain DAP. Higher-gravity fermentations require higher levels of yeast nutrients, so it is recommended that brewers try at least a few test fermentations with different levels of yeast nutrients to find the minimal effective dosage.

PROCESSING AIDS

In some cases, the fermented sugar solution will need to be stripped of unwanted aromas, flavors, or colors. This may involve filtration through activated carbon or using activated carbon as a fining agent. Filtration is greatly preferred because fining with activated carbon creates dust in the brewhouse and is hard to clear from the fined beverage. Alternatively, it may also involve other fining agents, either singly or sequentially.

FLAVORINGS

Flavorings for hard seltzers may be natural or artificial. They generally come as liquids, but some powders exist. Commercial breweries need to be aware of the relevant TTB and FDA regulations. The TTB and FDA websites have information on what is approved for malt beverages and beers (several useful links are given in chapter 6). In some cases, flavorings may be limited to a certain concentration; or the presence of an ingredient may require a warning label, as with beverages containing ingredients that include FD&C Yellow 5.

Manufacturers of flavorings advertise whether their ingredients are TTB and FDA compliant, so this is just a matter of checking. Performing an online search for "TTB approved ingredients" or "FDA approved ingredients" brings up a wide variety of companies selling flavor extracts. And, of course, companies that sell brewing ingredients to commercial brewers will carry TTB and FDA approved ingredients.

The most popular flavorings in hard seltzers include citrus and fruit flavors. In their natural form, the fruits in question will have a normal level of sweetness and acidity associated with them. The flavor extracts need not. In almost all cases, the level of sweetness will be lower in a hard seltzer. For example, dark cherry hard seltzers are not as sweet as cherries. For citrus-flavored hard seltzers, the level of acidity will likewise be lower. Lime-flavored hard seltzers are not as tart as an actual lime. When formulating recipes, it is important to run trials to determine the level of flavoring to use in a beverage with a level of sweetness, added acidity, and carbonation similar to your planned hard seltzer. Those three variables will affect how the flavoring is perceived.

Flavoring manufacturers will give a recommended dosage range, but brewers should blend the flavoring with non-alcoholic seltzer water or "blank" hard seltzer to determine the proper rate. Hard seltzers are less intensely flavored than many flavored beverages, so the recommended rate of addition for beverages might be too high unless it specifies it is the rate for hard seltzers. When testing for the appropriate flavoring levels, brewers should test for the proper levels of added acids. In most cases, fruit flavoring is added at a rate of 0.7–3.0 mL/L. This is equivalent to 2.8–12 fl. oz. (86–355 mL) per barrel. For less strongly flavored fruits, the rate may be higher. One brand of blueberry flavoring, for example, recommends a dosage of 6.0–8.0 mL/L. Even at these high dosages, the addition of flavoring changes the volume of the beverage very little. In the case of the example blueberry flavoring at its highest dosage, the added volume is only 0.8% of the total. Still, the brewer should account for this addition in their volume and alcohol by volume calculations.

ACIDS

The flavor of a hard seltzer may be improved by adding a small amount of the appropriate acid. Citric acid ($C_6H_8O_7$), for example, may improve the flavor of any hard seltzer with the flavor of any citrus fruit. Malic acid ($C_4H_6O_5$) may enhance the flavor of hard seltzers flavored with fruits in which malic acid is abundant. These include cherries, blueberries, and peaches. Both of these acids are available as white crystals. Fruit flavoring may already contain the appropriate acid to accentuate its flavor, so brewers should test the flavoring alone and next to samples treated with small concentrations of acid. Hard seltzers are never sour from acid additions but do have enough acidity to give the product a little "zing."

Citric acid may be present in the juice of citrus fruits at concentrations around 47 g/L. In limes, citric acid comprises 8% of the dry weight of the fruit. In apple juice, malic acid is present at a concentration of 5 g/L. The final concentrations in hard seltzers will be much lower as these beverages are less flavorful (and sweet) than fruit juices—and especially less tangy than lemon or lime juice. In addition, as mentioned, the flavoring itself may already contain some amount of the proper acid. Thus, acid additions required for hard seltzers may be as low as 1 g/L. The taste tests that brewers conduct to determine the rate of flavoring addition should be accompanied by tests of acid additions to the preferred flavor concentration.

The typical pH of a hard seltzer is 3.1 to 3.3. This low pH helps with the biological stability of the beverage. A small amount of acid may also be added prior to fermentation to lower the pH of the sugar solution to a range that the yeast prefers. For brewer's yeast, this is pH 5.0–5.5. For wine yeast, a pH around 3.8 is preferred.

CARBON DIOXIDE

Carbon dioxide (CO_2), as all brewers know, is a flavorless and odorless gas at temperatures and pressures encountered in breweries and inside packaged fermented beverages. (It is a liquid inside CO_2 tanks, which are highly pressurized, and a solid [dry ice] when very cold at atmospheric pressures.)

In an aqueous solution, a small amount of CO_2 combines with water to form carbonic acid, H_2CO_3. Carbonic acid is a weak acid. The hydration equilibrium constant, K_h, for carbonic acid in water at 25°C is

$$\frac{[H_2CO_3]}{[CO_2]} = K_h$$
$$= 1.7 \times 10^{-3}.$$

What this means is, in solution, very little of the total CO_2 is hydrated to carbonic acid.

However, hard seltzers are not at standard ambient temperature and pressure, and the concentration of carbonic acid increases with the partial pressure of CO_2 above a solution. In addition, the concentration of carbonic acid increases at lower pH levels. At the partial pressure of CO_2 in the atmosphere, the formation of carbonic acid contributes to lowering the pH of pure water to 5.7. In fact, this is the typical pH of raindrops. (For comparison, however, it's not the typical pH of standing water on Earth's surface. That water has dissolved acids, bases, buffers, and living organisms that all influence their pH. The pH of natural waters varies greatly but most bodies of water fall in the pH 6.5 to 8.5 range.) At CO_2 pressures typical of beer and soda, carbonic acid, and a nearly equal amount of bicarbonate (HCO_3^-) contribute to achieving a fairly low pH (3.7) in pure water. Bicarbonate (HCO_3^-) is the ion formed when carbonic acid gives up one proton. However, as discussed above, carbonic acid is not the only acid contributing to the acidity of hard seltzers. And these stronger acids are used in higher concentrations. So, although it is good know that CO_2 forms a small amount of carbonic acid (and bicarbonate) when dissolved in water, this knowledge does not have much effect on how hard seltzers are brewed.

Canned hard seltzers should be carbonated to 2.8 volumes of CO_2. Given the higher level of carbonation, bottling should only be done in bottles rated to accept that level without breaking. Brewpub brewers may decide to only carbonate their hard seltzers to the same degree as their beers in order to sidestep potential problems with their draught system.

You can think of hard seltzers as having two major ingredients: water and the sugars that are fermented by yeast. Because hard seltzer is typically lightly flavored, special attention must be paid to the quality of your brewing water. Most hard seltzers also have several minor ingredients. These include flavorings, sugar (for back sweetening), acid, stabilizing agents, and, in some cases, malt and hops. The yeast requires yeast nutrients to function properly and carbon dioxide is important enough to the character of the beverage—especially its level of fizziness—that it can be thought of as an ingredient. After fermentation, but before the flavoring and other ingredients are added, the neutral base may need to be cleaned up with the help of some processing aids.

© Brewers Association/Luke Trautwein

4

CRAFT BREWERY HARD SELTZER PRODUCTION

THERE ARE VARIATIONS IN HOW small commercial breweries make hard seltzers. Different breweries are set up differently, use different formulas, and take different approaches. However, despite differences in equipment and approach, all procedures for brewing hard seltzers share several core steps. In this chapter I will give a basic approach to making a hard seltzer, with the most common options discussed.

SUGAR PLUS WATER

The first step in making a hard seltzer is to mix the sugar solution. For this you need water, sugar, and a vessel to mix them in. Eventually, the sugar solution will need to be boiled (or at least heated). So, if you can mix the sugar solution in your kettle, do so. However, for some brewers the mash tun with its mixers is going to be the best choice. The solubility of sucrose at 77°F (25°C) is 2,000 g/L, and that for glucose is 909 g/L. Even for high-gravity sugar solutions, which will be diluted later, you will only be adding about one-eighth of this amount, or one-fourth if you are using glucose. What is more, the solubility increases at higher temperatures. So, dissolving the sugar takes time, but it will all dissolve with few problems in a vessel that can be stirred while the sugar is being added.

Initially, you should add slightly less water to the tank than the batch size, perhaps 28 gal. (106 L) per every barrel (117 L) expected. When planning how much water to add to your mixing vessel, know that 13.5 lb. (6.12 kg) of sugar displaces 1.0 gal. (3.8 L) of water. This is equivalent to 419 lb. of sugar displacing 1.0 US barrel of liquid or 162 kg of sugar displacing a hectoliter of liquid. After the sugar is dissolved, you can top up to the batch size plus the volume that a 15-minute boil (or pasteurization step) will evaporate. Treat the water to remove chlorine compounds as you would for any brewing liquor. Additionally, you may want to add minerals (yielding 50–100 ppm Ca^{2+}) to make the water taste better, although this is probably only necessary if distilled or RO water is being used. Ideally, the water should contain no more than 50 ppm HCO_3^-.

So, if you heat the water as you are stirring in the sugar it should dissolve quickly. This is especially true if you add the sugar in aliquots and allow each to dissolve completely before adding the next. If added too quickly, it is possible for clumps of dry sugar crystals to be surrounded by water and resist being dissolved, at least for a time. These will float on top of the solution initially, then sink when water begins to dissolve into their interior. If they come to rest on a heated surface they can scorch—this will add color and flavor to the sugar mix and should be avoided. Due to the high solubility of sugar, however, getting it into solution should not require any extraordinary steps.

Sugar is not a hazardous substance. You would not, for example, take any safety precautions if you were using it in your kitchen. However, when using the amounts called for in hard seltzers, the material safety data sheet (MSDS) for the sugar you are using should be consulted. In the case of sucrose or glucose, handlers should wear goggles, gloves, and a dust mask. In addition, the area where you are handling the sugar should be well ventilated because the dust particles are crystals that can mechanically irritate the eye and cause skin irritation. The Occupational Safety and Health Administration (OSHA) gives the personal exposure limit (PEL) of sucrose dust as a time-weighted average (TWA) of 5 mg/m³ for the respirable fraction of the dust. Overall, however, handling sucrose in an industrial setting is not particularly hazardous. It is, however, sticky if it gets wet.

If sugar dust or spilled sugar settles anywhere in the brewhouse it should be cleaned immediately. If it becomes wet it will become very sticky and provide a carbon source for microorganisms to grow. When adding sugar to your mixing vessel, try to minimize the amount of dust that escapes and the amount that is spilled. Clean up any spills or settled dust immediately. Hot water will easily rinse any surface. Handling sugar in a small brewery usually involves lugging sacks of sugar onto the brewing platform in the brewhouse. Larger breweries may want to invest in specialized equipment to handle the movement of sugar.

By the time the sugar is dissolved, the solution should already be heated a bit. At this point, you should add water to bring the solution up to the appropriate volume for the boil. The next step is to transfer it to the kettle.

If you are going to adjust the pH of the solution, this is the time to do it. Beer wort is generally around pH 5.0 after the boil, so this is a good value to target if you are using brewer's yeast. Wine yeast generally starts operating at a lower value, around pH 3.8. Adjust the pH with food-grade phosphoric acid or lactic acid. A solution of just water and sucrose or glucose has no buffering capacity, so very little acid should be required unless the water is high in carbonates. The amount of acid required depends on the mineral content of your water. Add small amounts of acid—a few fluid ounces per barrel, or roughly 50 mL per hectoliter—stir, and then test the pH, repeating as needed. And know that you do not need to hit a pH of 5.0 exactly, anything in the ballpark is fine. The boil will not alter the pH as it does during wort production. The pH drop in wort is driven by reactions between calcium and phosphates, whereas your sugar solution will not contain any phosphates. Also keep in mind that pH is temperature dependent, so cool your sample to the appropriate temperature for your pH meter when testing. Most pH meters are calibrated to 77°F (25°C) or "room temperature." Some meters may feature automatic temperature compensation (ATC).

Mash for a Malt Beverage

Hard seltzers brewed as a malt beverage under the TTB's classification must contain 25% malt and a small amount (7.5 lbs/100 bbl., or 29 g/hL) of hops. (Under the TTB's classification scheme, brewing with malt and no hops would make it a beer.) Production of a malt beverage begins with a small mash of very-low-color malt. Any color added by the malt will need to be removed later. A step mash with a long rest at 140–145°F (60–63°C) may be employed to generate a very fermentable wort. In addition, an exogenous enzyme, such as amyloglucosidase, may be added to reduce any residual complex carbohydrates to simple sugars. While the mash is proceeding, the brewer may mix the sugar and water solution in the kettle, which should at most be three-quarters full to leave room for the wort. After the mash, the wort can be pumped to the kettle to be boiled.

BOILING AND COOLING

The sugar solution is usually boiled for a short time and then cooled before fermentation. Alternatively, the sugar solution may be heated to 170°F (77°C) and held for 15 minutes. The goal of the boil is simply to sanitize the solution. If any unwanted volatile compounds are present in the sugar solution, the boil will drive these off. Even if you are brewing a malt beverage—which must include malt and hops—you do not want to isomerize any alpha acids in your hops. As mentioned in chapter 3, spent hops or even hop leaves (not cones) may be used to ensure that no bitterness is imparted. Additionally, there is no requirement for the hops to be boiled for any length of time. They may be added at knockout or when the "wort" is whirlpooled, if it is. Boiling the sugar solution for a short time will not caramelize any of the sugar nor add color to the solution. The temperature required to caramelize sucrose or glucose is 320°F (160°C) or above and this cannot be arrived at when boiling a (relatively) dilute sugar solution in bulk. However, if clumps of incompletely dissolved sugar make it into the kettle they may settle on a hot surface and scorch.

Boil (or heat) the sugar solution for 15 minutes, sufficient to reduce the pre-boil volume slightly to your batch size. Add yeast nutrients such as DAP near the beginning of the boil. If you are using yeast nutrients that contain vitamins, reserve them for later as the vitamins can be destroyed by the heat of the boil. If you are brewing a malt beverage, you will have a hop addition at some point during the boil, before proceeding directly to cooling. There is no need for whirlpooling unless your water has a high level of carbonates, you added hops, or sediment of any type is present. Nothing should be precipitating in the boil of a solution consisting of only sugar and water. The sugar solution needs to be cooled, aerated, and transferred to a fermentor.

If you are using a yeast strain you normally use for beer production, cool the sugar solution to the usual temperature and aerate to the same degree. For most ale strains, something around 65–68°F (18–20°C) and 6–8 ppm of oxygen should be close to optimal. For high-gravity fermentations, up to 12 ppm of oxygen may be required.

FERMENTATION

Fermentation is the make-or-break stage of a hard seltzer. This stage is almost universally regarded as the most difficult part of making a hard seltzer. Running an ordered fermentation will save you effort later and ultimately make a better product. The key to running a fermentation well—beyond the variables that apply to ordinary beer fermentations—is adding the appropriate level of yeast and yeast nutrients. It may take you several test batches to get the balance right and you may need to refine your approach as you gain more experience.

If you are fermenting your hard seltzer at working strength, pitch the yeast. If you are using brewer's yeast, your pitching rate should be in line with your normal pitching rate, or perhaps up to 20% higher. If you are using a wine yeast, follow the cell counts recommended for it. (Note that, as a commercial brewer, you cannot call your hard seltzer gluten-free if you used a solution containing malt to propagate your yeast for pitching.)

At working strength, the fermentation may last a little longer than a typical beer fermentation at the same starting gravity, but not by much. High-gravity fermentations may take longer. Fermentation times of 8–11 days are common. And, of course, if the yeast does not have the required amount of nutrients the fermentation may proceed even more slowly. A sluggish fermentation is almost guaranteed if yeast nutrition is not addressed properly. As mentioned in chapter 3, you may need between 250 and 300 ppm of FAN to yield an orderly fermentation. As with beer fermentations, the yeast strain, the level of aeration, and density of solution to be fermented all influence the level of nutrients required. The yeast manufacturer may have data on the appropriate level of FAN required for your yeast. Some distiller's yeast preparations are packaged with the appropriate amount of nutrients. You should achieve at least one successful test fermentation before proceeding to try a production-scale batch.

Presuming you estimated the amount of yeast nutrients correctly (or followed the manufacturer's recommendations), the fermentation should proceed in an orderly fashion and finish at an appropriately low density of around −1.8°Bx to −2.0°Bx. There are hydrometers that have scales that measure down to −3°Bx to −5°Bx, which may come in handy for brewers hard seltzers, as well as brut IPAs. You should hold your fermentation temperature steady, perhaps raising it to the top end of your yeast strain's working temperature range at the very end of fermentation. A late rise in temperature should not lead to ester formation to the degree it would in early fermentation. Stirring the tank, if you have that option, can also help. All you need is a couple minutes of stirring twice a day. If a fermentation is nearing the end but seems sluggish, try taking the pH of the solution. Most yeast strains struggle if the pH drops below 3.5. An overly low pH may be corrected by adding sodium bicarbonate (baking soda) to neutralize some of the acid. If this is a recurring problem, your water chemistry should be adjusted pre-fermentation to include enough carbonates to buffer the solution a bit, as is done in some mead fermentations.

If you ferment a high-gravity sugar solution, with the intention of diluting it to working strength before packaging, you may have more difficulty with your fermentation. However, this is not insurmountable. When fermenting a high-gravity solution, make sure you are pitching the proper amount of yeast. A minimum of 1 million cells per mL per degree Plato—the old-school ale pitching rate recommendation—is required. Twenty to 50 percent more cells than this is likely better. Another thing you may need to do to help fermentation along is give the yeast a second shot of oxygen after pitching. But do this before high kräusen—aerating after high kräusen is not recommended as this could stimulate the production of more diacetyl than the yeast can reabsorb later.

Breaking the yeast nutrients into two aliquots, or perhaps even three, and adding them sequentially is also an option. The idea here is to give the yeast nutrients as they are needed, not all up front. One way to stagger yeast nutrient additions would be to add half (or up to two-thirds) of the yeast nutrients during the boil, then add the remaining nutrients at high kräusen. Be sure not to add yeast nutrients with vitamins during the boil. Another option would be to add half the yeast nutrients in the boil, another quarter (of the total) right before high kräusen, and the remaining one-quarter the day after high kräusen. Adding yeast nutrients late in the fermentation is not recommended as any unused nutrients can lead to biological instability in the final product and will need to be scrubbed by filtration or fining.

If you want to ferment a high-gravity sugar solution beyond what your yeast would normally be able to handle, you may want to consider "feeding" the fermentation. The basic idea is to begin fermenting a sugar solution at a concentration the yeast can handle well. When the specific gravity drops, add a little more sugar, all the while keeping the specific gravity within levels the yeast can handle well. Feeding complicates the fermentation and should really only be considered if nothing else works or if you are set on fermenting a very high gravity sugar solution.

As an example, let us say you want to ferment 30 bbl. of a 16°Bx sugar solution. Test batches have shown that your yeast performs well on batches up to 12°Bx but runs into problems at higher gravities. Your first step is to calculate the total sugar amount of sugar you would need to produce 30 bbl. with a starting gravity of 16°Bx. We will call that amount $S_{(30\_16)}$. Next, calculate how much sugar it would take to make roughly ⅞ of that volume (i.e., ~26 bbl.) with a starting gravity of 12°Bx. We will call that amount $S_{(26\_12)}$. Subtracting the latter from the former gives you how much additional sugar you will need to bring the batch to a virtual starting gravity of 16°Bx. We can call that difference

$S_{(feeding)}$. When calculating these variables, you must use the same volume and mass units for all three variables, whether barrels, gallons, pounds, ounces, liters, kilograms, or other.

With these values in hand, you begin by brewing and starting to ferment your "short" batch of 12°Bx sugar solution from $S_{(26\_12)}$. Once it reaches 8°Bx, make a sugar solution with the remaining sugar (i.e., $S_{(feeding)}$) to a volume ⅛ of your total batch size. (If your initial batch size was some fraction other than ⅞ of the total batch size, the feeding volume plus your short batch volume should equal your total volume.) Blend the feeding solution with the 8°Bx fermenting short batch. This will bring the gravity of the fermenting batch up to 12°Bx, the virtual starting gravity up to 16°Bx, and the volume up to your total batch volume. Note that the sugar solution used for feeding will be at a very high gravity, but still well below the solubility level of sucrose. When adding the feeding solution to the main fermenting batch do not aerate either the main batch or the feeding solution. Adding oxygen at this point will trigger the production of diacetyl. Likewise, do not add further yeast nutrients.

As an option, you can do two feedings, each at the same gravity but half the volume as before. Doing this will put less stress on the yeast. For the first feeding, let the short batch fermentation proceed to 10°Bx, then boost it back to 12°Bx with the feeding solution. Repeat with the second feeding, with this final addition bringing the virtual starting gravity to 16°Bx and the volume to the full batch size.

As with working strength fermentations, letting the temperature rise at the very end of fermentation and intermittently stirring the tank may also help—in fact, it may be required. Expect a high-gravity fermentation to last longer than an equivalent beer fermentation, and substantially longer than a hard seltzer working-strength fermentation. Fermentations lasting three weeks, or even a month, have been reported. These are problematic, however, and a well-run fermentation should finish within 8–11 days.

High-gravity neutral bases eventually need to be blended down to working strength with de-aerated water, but that does not happen until after they are cleaned up.

CLEAN UP

The neutral malt base for a hard seltzer is expected to be free of aroma, flavor, and color. Often, the brewer must clean the base up for this to be the case. The first stage of clean up involves filtration, fining, or centrifugation to yield a clear solution that is free of yeast cells and other large particles.

This step cleans up the neutral base to the extent that an ordinary beer would be clarified. If does not, however, remove aromas, flavors, or color. In order to achieve the clarity and lack of color seen in hard seltzer, other methods are required.

At the largest breweries, the removal of aroma, flavor, and even color may be accomplished by ultrafiltration or reverse osmosis (RO). In both these processes, the fermented base is pressed against a semipermeable membrane. The membrane allows water molecules and ethanol molecules to pass through, but the pore size is small enough that odorants, flavor-active molecules, and pigments or other colored substances are left behind. This will produce a crystal clear, colorless base solution.

Smaller breweries that do not have ultrafiltration or RO equipment can filter their neutral base through activated carbon or recirculate the solution over a bed of granular activated carbon. Fining with activated carbon will also work, but it is very dusty and can be extremely difficult to remove from solution. Both granular and powdered forms of activated carbon should be thoroughly rinsed with clean water prior to use.

Carbon filtration can remove odors, flavors, and colors. Carbon sheet filters come in different filtration depths and pores sizes and are designed to fit into a frame. Everything from coarse filtration to sterile filtration can be achieved with carbon filters. Deeper depths and smaller pore sizes clean the neutral base more effectively but require more filtration time for the liquid to pass through. A filter with a depth of around 4 mm and a pore size between 1 and 25 micrometers would be a good trade-off for a brewery. The up-front cost of carbon filtration is higher than fining with activated carbon. However, carbon filters create substantially less mess in the brewery. To save on the cost of carbon filter pads, you should only run clear neutral base through the filter rack, that is, neutral base that has already gone through the first stage of clean up with "ordinary" filtration, fining, or centrifugation.

Brewers can also fine with activated carbon. Rates of 50–2,000 mg/L (equivalent to 5.8–230 g/bbl.) are common, with the lower end of the range being useful for removing odors and the higher end of the range for stripping color. Typically, a stock solution of 10% (w/v) activated carbon is mixed before stirring it into the main batch. The activated carbon must be stirred thoroughly into the neutral base. It will settle out in an hour or two.

Activated carbon is dusty and brewers should only use it in a well-ventilated area, always wear goggles and a dust mask while handling it, and avoid skin contact. In addition, using activated carbon for fining creates a black sludge that must be cleaned after the tank is emptied. If not completely removed from solution it can leave the beverage with a gray cast.

If the neutral base contains odors, bubbling CO_2 through the solution can knock them out of solution. The most common off-odor encountered in hard seltzer production is hydrogen sulfide (H_2S), which can smell like rotten eggs or a burnt match. Bubbling CO_2 through the mixture will not remove flavors or colors. Keep in mind that the neutral base will be saturated with CO_2 immediately after fermentation. Stirring the tank before the treatment will knock some of the gas out of solution. This, in combination with beginning the treatment with just a trickle of CO_2 gas, will minimize the risk of a violent bubbling over.

Although a neutral base can be scrubbed of odor, flavor, and color, you should endeavor to produce the cleanest neutral base possible to begin with. This will minimize the number of filtration passes or amount of fining required.

DILUTION

If a strong neutral base was brewed, that is, one with a higher alcohol content than that intended for the beverage, it will have to be diluted to working strength. Use de-aerated water for this dilution. In the largest breweries, designed for producing high-gravity beer that is diluted to working strength at packaging, it may be possible to obtain water containing as little oxygen as 80 parts per billion. Smaller breweries typically do not have the equipment to do this. Simple boiling for 15 minutes should reduce the level of oxygen—usually 8–9 ppm in water at room temperature and atmospheric pressure—to less than 1 ppm. Bubbling CO_2 through the solution will also bump out oxygen (and other gases).

The volume of strong neutral base and de-aerated water required for any dilution step can be calculated if the desired ABV is known. Use the equation

$$C_1V_1 = C_2V_2.$$

In the above equation, C_1 and C_2 are the concentrations (i.e., % ABV) of the starting solution and end solution, respectively. Likewise, V_1 and V_2 are the starting volume and end volume, respectively.

As an example, suppose you have 7 bbl. of neutral base at 12% ABV and wanted to fill a 3.5 bbl. tank with 4% ABV neutral base. You need to calculate V_1, the amount of strong neutral base you have to take to dilute to 3.5 bbl. of working strength neutral base.

Figure 4.1 Overview of hard seltzer process

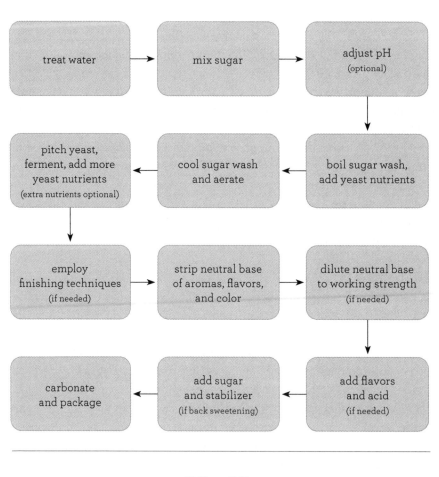

$$C_1 V_1 = C_2 V_2$$
$$12 \cdot V_1 = 4 \cdot 3.5$$
$$V_1 = (4 \cdot 3.5)/12$$
$$= 14/12$$
$$= 1.16$$

Solving for V_1 yields 1.16, so 1.16 bbl. of 12% ABV base is required. As such, 1.16 bbl. subtracted from 3.5 bbl. means 2.34 bbl. of de-aerated water is required for dilution.

Available tank space should be considered before brewing a strong neutral base so that, when diluted, the resulting hard seltzers fill their respective tanks.

To give a simple example, if you had two 15 bbl. brite tanks you wished to fill with 5% ABV hard seltzers, and one 15 bbl. fermentor available, brewing 15 bbl. of a 10% ABV strong neutral base would, after dilution, fill both brite tanks completely without any left over.

FINAL BLENDING

In the blending stage, the neutral malt base is transformed into a flavored hard seltzer. This is simply a matter of mixing the appropriate flavors and acids with the working strength base. If the beverage is going to be back sweetened, the sugar is also added. If not pasteurizing after back sweetening, a stabilizer or preservative should also be added—potassium sorbate is recommended. Also, sometimes citric acid is added to lower the pH to the 3.0–3.1 range, further stabilizing the beverage. Whenever adding multiple solids to any liquid, do not mix the solids. Stir each one into solution in succession, ensuring each is thoroughly dissolved before proceeding to the next.

The flavoring agent for a hard seltzer is most likely a liquid, although some are powders. The acid (if required) will be in the form of white crystals or a clear liquid. Although the amounts required are very small relative to the batch size, wearing gloves, goggles, and a dust mask are recommended when handling flavoring agents and acids. Add each component separately rather than mixing them together and then stirring them into the main batch. Once all the materials are dissolved into the batch, it should be carbonated to 2.8 volumes of CO_2. If the hard seltzer is going to be served on draught, carbonate it to the usual level the draught system is balanced for. This is around 2.5 volumes of CO_2 for most brewpub systems.

PACKAGING

Hard seltzers are usually canned, by convention in cans that are taller and narrower than normal beer or soda cans. These are called sleek style cans. Brewers should conduct corrosion tests on the cans they select, as hard seltzers can have a low pH (down to 3.0). Brewpubs may serve hard seltzer through their draught system. Brewers that do so should keep a line dedicated to hard seltzer because the fruit flavoring may soak into the tubing, tainting any beer that is later pushed through the same line.

Conceptually, making a hard seltzer is not difficult. As with anything, paying attention to the details will increase your chances of success dramatically. Many of the fundamentals to making good beer—proper pitching rate, proper wort aeration, running an ordered fermentation—also apply to making hard seltzer. The fermentation is what requires the most attention. A solution of plain sugar and water does not have the nutrients required to support the yeast. If yeast nutrients are not supplied, the fermentation will stall before it reaches a reasonable terminal gravity. Stress on the yeast may also lead to off-aromas. However, although adequate yeast nutrition is absolutely required, an overly large addition of yeast nutrients has negative consequences as well. There is a "window" of correct yeast nutrient amounts for every combination of yeast strain and starting gravity. If you have matched your yeast nutrients to your yeast and sugar base gravity, the fermentation should proceed in an orderly manner. However, some fermentations may still require agitation, an additional dose of yeast nutrients, or the raising of the fermentor temperature so that they reach the finish line.

© Getty/LoveTheWind

5

RECIPES FOR CRAFT BREWERIES

IN THIS CHAPTER I GIVE recipes for most of the popular types of hard seltzer. The flavor of each is simply a matter of what flavoring extract is added, which can be changed to suit your needs. Although the required volume will differ between flavorings, the difference in amounts is small enough that it can be ignored (any difference typically works out to roughly 17 fl. oz. per barrel, or less than half a liter of flavoring per 117 liters). At the end of this chapter I also give recipes for two strong neutral bases that can be diluted to working strength.

Of course, it is not hard to formulate a hard seltzer from scratch, so let us start there. When formulating a hard seltzer recipe, you really only need to make four decisions. What is the alcoholic strength of the beverage? What is the flavor of the beverage? Will it be back sweetened? And, finally, will it be packaged in cans or served on draught? Based on the answers, some downstream decisions will need to be made, but these four are the main decision points.

The alcoholic strength of the beverage is correlated with its caloric content. Most hard seltzers weigh in a 4.0%–5.0% ABV and have 90–100 calories per 12 fl. oz. Almost all of those calories are from ethanol. Once the alcoholic strength is decided on, you need to decide if you will brew the beverage at working strength or make a strong neutral base and dilute it to working strength before adding the flavoring. The benefits of making a working strength base is that the yeast experiences less stress and the resulting fermentation is faster and cleaner than a high-gravity fermentation. You also do not need to prepare de-aerated water when a working strength base is brewed. The benefit of making a strong neutral base is that you can make a greater volume of hard seltzer utilizing the same amount of tank space.

Choosing the flavors for your hard seltzers is purely subjective. The most popular flavors are citrus fruits (lime, grapefruit, etc.) and other, non-citrus, fruits (cherry, pineapple, etc.), for which TTB-approved commercially produced extracts are available, among many more. If there is an ingredient with a local angle, making a hard seltzer featuring its flavor may be a smart business decision. However, depending on how common this ingredient is, you may need to use your own preparation of it to infuse the hard seltzer with flavor. You will also need to get TTB, and maybe FDA, approval to use the ingredient and its preparation in a commercially produced beverage.

The expression of the added flavor will be influenced by the acidity of the beverage and the level of sweetness and carbonation. You should conduct bench trials to determine whether the flavoring is improved with a small addition of the appropriate acid. The same goes for determining the appropriate level of back sweetening for the beverage. Keep in mind that sweetness is a flavor that most people find pleasing. As such, sweeter fruit-flavored beverages will taste better to most. However, beverages sweetened with sugar also contain more calories and carbohydrates, two things consumers want to be low in hard seltzers. The bench trials to determine flavoring levels, acidity levels, and back sweetening should be done with (soft) seltzer as the mixer because carbonation also influences flavor expression.

The level of flavoring in most mass-produced hard seltzers is low. For people accustomed to drinking high-quality craft beers, wines, or similar fermented beverages, the flavor of hard seltzers may seem lacking in big flavors and complexity. Hard seltzers might be described as eminently quaffable but somewhat forgettable. So do not worry if your hard seltzer is not bursting with fresh fruit flavor, that is not what fans of this beverage are expecting. In fact, given the amount of carbohydrates required to achieve that level of character—and the calories that would accompany them—a hard seltzer like this would likely be rejected in favor of a less flavorful, less caloric, version. Then again, if you want to stress the craft aspect of your brewery, there may be a niche for slightly higher-calorie hard seltzers that pack in more flavor.

As discussed in chapter 4, brewers who back sweeten their hard seltzers will also need to add a stabilizer. For smaller breweries, this will require the addition of potassium sorbate. Larger breweries can pasteurize their product.

If you package your hard seltzer in cans, the standard level of carbonation is 2.8 volumes of CO_2. If you plan to serve your hard seltzer through a draught system, either from kegs or from brewpub serving tanks, carbonating it to standard craft beer levels (2.5 volumes of CO_2) will lower the probability of experiencing problems when dispensing it.

Having made decisions on alcoholic strength, flavor, sweetening, and packaging, you can write out a trial recipe.

CONCENTRATION AND VOLUME

I give instructions on how to brew these hard seltzers at working strength. However, I also give the instructions starting with a volume of neutral base solution at a given alcohol level (in ABV). This is for brewers who wish to brew a strong neutral base and dilute it when it comes time to blend the hard seltzer components.

CALCULATING VOLUMES TO DILUTE

In order to dilute strong neutral bases into working strength neutral bases, you only need one equation:

$$C_1 V_1 = C_2 V_2.$$

We have already come across this equation in the "Dilution" section of chapter 4. In this equation, C is concentration and V is volume. The subscripts denote the two different solutions, "1" is the pre-dilution solution and "2" the post-dilution solution. This "concentration times volume" equation, known to every college chemistry major, will give you the right dilution factor every time.

For example, let us say you have a 40-barrel fermentor filled with a neutral base. The starting gravity is 1.060 and the calculated ethanol content is 7.6% ABV. How much 5.0% ABV hard seltzer can you make from that? Take your 7.6% solution at a volume of 40 barrels, which is your pre-dilution solution, and set it equal to your desired post-solution, which is 5% but at an unknown volume (V_2):

$$7.6 \cdot 40 = 5.0 \cdot V_2$$

Isolate the unknown quantity by dividing both sides of the equation by 5:

$$V_2 = (7.6 \cdot 40)/5.0$$
$$= 304/5.0$$
$$= 60.8$$

So, you can produce 60.8 barrels of 5% ABV hard seltzer from your 40 barrels of 7.6% ABV neutral base.

The odds are, however, that a brewery with 40-barrel fermentors is not going to have a 60-barrel tank for blending. What if the brewery only has 15-barrel brite tanks? Also, what if the owner wants to produce some 4% hard seltzer alongside the 5% hard seltzers to see if customers will pay the same price for a beverage with less ingredient cost? The concentration times volume equation comes to the rescue.

So, the owner wants at least one 4% ABV seltzer and your brite tanks are 15 barrels. As before, you have 40 bbl. of 7.6% ABV base. Take the desired 4% base times the volume it will occupy in the brite tank (15 bbl.) and set it equal to your neutral base at 7.6%. This time the unknown volume, V_2, is how much of the 7.6% base you need to make 15 bbl. of 4% hard seltzer.

$$4 \cdot 15 = 7.6 \cdot V_2$$
$$V_2 = (4 \cdot 15)/7.6$$
$$= 7.89$$

Solving for V_2 yields 7.9, which means you need 7.9 bbl. of 7.6% ABV neutral base to make 15 bbl. of 4% ABV seltzer. Now, how much 5% seltzer can you make with the remaining neutral base? Start by subtracting 7.9 barrels from 40 barrels, to yield 32 barrels of neutral base (I rounded to 32 bbl. here. In your own equations, you can carry out your calculations to as many decimal places as is justified by the accuracy of your volume measurements.)

Repeat the concentration times volume equation, this time for a 5% seltzer.

$$5 \cdot 15 = 7.6 \cdot V_2$$
$$V_2 = (5 \cdot 15)/7.6$$
$$= 9.87$$

In this case, V_2 equals 9.9. This means 9.9 barrels of your strong neutral base is needed to blend 15 bbl. of 5% seltzer. This leaves you with 22 bbl. of strong neutral base. This is enough to make 2.2 more 15-barrel batches of 5% hard seltzer (i.e., 22 bbl. divided by 9.9). So, that makes a total of 3 full batches of 5% seltzer, which leaves you with a remainder of 2.2 bbl. of the 7.6% base. What can be done with that? No problem, the concentration times volume equation can tell you. In this case you have 2.2 bbl. at 7.6%. That is 4.5 bbl. at 5% ABV. To blend that you would need:

$$7.6 \cdot 2.2 = 5 \cdot V_2$$
$$V_2 = (7.6 \cdot 2.2)/5$$
$$= 3.34$$

So, you could make 3.3 barrels of 5% hard seltzer with the last bit of the 7.6% strong neutral base.

CALCULATING THE STRENGTH FOR THE NEUTRAL BASE

Of course, making a small batch a hard seltzer to use up the last of your neutral base means one of your tanks ends up only partially filled. When you plan to brew your neutral base, it is best to think ahead to how many full tanks of finished hard seltzer you desire. Then, brew the neutral base to a volume and strength such that it will be diluted into this number. This is very easy to do. Start by deciding how much hard seltzer you want and sum the total volume of the tanks that will hold it. Now, use the $C_1 V_1 = C_2 V_2$ equation, but this time you know the volumes of your brite tanks and fermentor, so you calculate the percent ABV that your neutral base should be.

For example, let us say you have three 15 bbl. brite tanks and a 30 bbl. fermentor. You want to fill all three brites with 5% ABV hard seltzer, which is 45 bbl. altogether. Plugging those figures into the equation:

$$C_1 V_1 = C_2 V_2$$
$$5 \cdot 45 = C_2 \cdot 30$$
$$C_2 = (5 \cdot 45)/30$$
$$= 7.5$$

The calculation shows you should brew a 7.5% ABV neutral base in your 30 bbl. fermentor.

RECIPES

This section contains eight recipes for hard seltzers of varying strengths. I have also included two recipes for strong neutral sugar bases that can be diluted to make larger volumes of hard seltzer. As this chapter is for professional brewers, I give 1.0 bbl. (117 L) recipes. To scale the recipe for your brewery, simply multiply all the ingredients in the one-barrel recipe by your brewhouse size. (Do not worry, homebrewers, there are five-gallon [19 L] recipes in chapter 8.) Each recipe specifies a certain volume of neutral base at a given alcoholic content. This can be obtained either by diluting a strong neutral base—as described above—or by fermenting a sugar solution at working strength.

I have tried to put a number to everything. However, some ingredients are added "to taste" because they really do need the brewer's input. Likewise, the amount of phosphoric acid required for pH adjustment depends both on the mineral content of your water and your pH target. This needs to be added in small amounts and tested to hit the proper pH.

I would highly recommend doing a pilot brew of any hard seltzer before jumping into a full production batch.

HARD SELTZER RECIPES

STANDARD 4% ABV
HARD SELTZER *For 1 US barrel (31 gal., or 117 L)*

Calories per serving: 90
Flavor: lime

SELTZER INGREDIENTS
31 gal. (117 L) 4.0% ABV neutral base
5.9 fl. oz. (175 mL) lime flavoring
citric acid (to taste)
12 oz. (340 g) sucrose
0.81 oz. (23 g) potassium sorbate (necessary if not pasteurizing)

4% NEUTRAL BASE INGREDIENTS
21.5 lb. (9.75 kg) sucrose
phosphoric acid (for pH adjustment)
700 billion cells yeast
1.3 oz. (37 g) yeast nutrients

PROCEDURES FOR SELTZER

Dilute an appropriate amount of your strong neutral base to the desired number of barrels at 4% ABV. Or brew the neutral base with the amount of sugar listed (per barrel). Add the flavoring, acid (if needed), and sugar for back sweetening. If you are not going to pasteurize the hard seltzer, add the potassium sorbate. Carbonate to 2.8 volumes of CO_2 if canning or to the level of CO_2 appropriate for your draught system in that case. Package (in cans or kegs) or pump to serving tanks.

PROCEDURES FOR 4% NEUTRAL BASE

If you are fermenting your neutral base at working strength, follow these instructions. Fill your mash tun with 27.0 gal. (102 L) of water (per barrel). Add the correct amount of sugar (per barrel) to your mash tun and stir until dissolved. Add water to top up to your desired volume. Check with a hydrometer or refractometer, it should read 1.032 SG, or 8.0°Bx. Check the pH and adjust to an appropriate pH for your yeast, if desired. (This is around pH 5 for beer yeasts or pH 3.8 for wine yeasts.)

Pump the sugar slurry to your kettle and boil or hold the solution at 170°F (77°C) for 15 minutes. Cool to an appropriate temperature for your yeast strain. (For ale yeasts, cool to around 65°F, or 18°C.) Transfer the cooled sugar solution to your fermentor. (Repeat as needed to fill your fermentor.)

Aerate the mixture in the fermentor, pitch the yeast, and add yeast nutrients. Ferment in a temperature range that will produce a fast fermentation, but one that will not produce excessive esters or other yeast characters. This temperature depends on the yeast strain. For most neutral ale strains, 65–68°F (18–20°C) will work. Wine strains can ferment at much higher temperatures, up to 80°F (27°C). Monitor the specific gravity daily to ensure that fermentation is proceeding at a reasonable pace. If the fermentation slows beyond what it normally does early on, or the yeast is producing unusual amounts of sulfur or other by-products, a second dose of yeast nutrients may be called for. This should be ⅛–¼ the amount listed in the ingredients list. As the fermentation nears its conclusion, you may want to stir the tank gently for a few minutes per day or allow the temperature to rise slightly. Do not exceed the yeast strain's recommended working temperature range.

After fermentation, you may want to bubble CO_2 through your tanks to scrub any unwanted aromas. Likewise, you may want to either fine with activated carbon or filter your hard seltzer base through activated carbon (filtering methods are easier to work with and less messy than fining). The amount of bubbling and carbon used will depend on how clean the 4% base is. With proper yeast nutrition, fermenting a low-gravity solution such as this should not put much stress on the yeast. Once your base is brewed and cleaned up, add the remaining ingredients as described above in the seltzer ingredients and procedures.

STANDARD 5% ABV
HARD SELTZER *For 1 US barrel (31 gal., or 117 L)*

Calories per serving: 100
Flavor: cherry

SELTZER INGREDIENTS
31 gal. (117 L) 5.0% ABV neutral base
5.1 fl. oz. (150 mL) cherry flavoring
malic acid (to taste)
12 oz. (340 g) sucrose
0.81 oz. (23 g) potassium sorbate (necessary if not pasteurizing)

5% NEUTRAL BASE INGREDIENTS
27.0 b. (12.3 kg) sucrose
phosphoric acid (for pH adjustment)
880 billion cells yeast
1.4 oz. (40 g) yeast nutrients

PROCEDURES FOR SELTZER
Dilute an appropriate amount of your strong neutral base to the desired number of barrels at 5% ABV. Or brew the neutral base with the amount of sugar listed (per barrel). Add the flavoring, acid (if needed), and sugar. If you are not going to pasteurize the hard seltzer, add the potassium sorbate. Carbonate to 2.8 volumes of CO_2 if canning or to the level of CO_2 appropriate for your draught system in that case. Package (in cans or kegs) or pump to serving tanks.

PROCEDURES FOR 5% NEUTRAL BASE
If you are fermenting your neutral base at working strength, follow these instructions. Fill your mash tun with 27.0 gallons (102 L) of water (per barrel). Add the correct amount of sugar (per barrel) to your mash tun and stir until dissolved. Add water to to top up to your desired volume. Check with a hydrometer or refractometer, the density should be 1.040 SG, or 10°Bx. Check the pH and adjust to an appropriate pH for your yeast, if desired. (This is around pH 5 for beer yeasts or pH 4 for wine yeasts.)

Pump the sugar slurry to your kettle and boil or hold the solution at 170°F (77°C) for 15 minutes. Cool to an appropriate temperature for your yeast strain. (For ale yeasts, cool to around 65°F, or 18°C.) Transfer the cooled sugar solution to your fermentor. (Repeat as needed to fill your fermentor.)

Aerate the mixture in the fermentor, pitch the yeast, and add yeast nutrients. Ferment in a temperature range that will produce a fast fermentation, but one that will not produce excessive esters or other yeast characters. For most neutral ale strains, 65–68°F (18–20°C) will work. Wine strains can ferment at much higher temperatures, up to 80°F (27°C). Monitor the specific gravity daily to ensure that fermentation is proceeding in an orderly manner. If the fermentation slows beyond what it normally does early on, or the yeast is producing unusual amounts of sulfur or other by-products, a second dose of yeast nutrients may be called for. This should be ⅛–¼ the amount listed in the ingredients list. As the fermentation nears its conclusion, you may want to stir the tank gently for a few minutes per day or allow the temperature to rise slightly. Do not exceed the yeast strain's recommended working temperature range.

After fermentation, you may want to bubble CO_2 through your tanks to scrub any unwanted aromas. Likewise, you may want to either fine with activated carbon or filter your hard seltzer base through activated carbon (filtering methods are easier to work with and less messy than fining). The amount of bubbling and carbon used will depend on how clean the 5% base is. With proper yeast nutrition, fermenting a low-gravity solution such as this should not put much stress on the yeast. Once your base is brewed and cleaned up, proceed to adding the remaining ingredients as described above in the seltzer ingredients and procedures.

SLIGHTLY SWEET 4% ABV
HARD SELTZER *For 1 US barrel (31 gal., or 117 L)*

Calories per serving: 99
Flavor: peach

SELTZER INGREDIENTS
31 gal. (117 L) 4.0% ABV neutral base
12.7 fl. oz. (375 mL) peach flavoring
malic acid (to taste)
50 oz. (1.4 kg) sucrose
0.81 oz. (23 g) potassium sorbate (necessary if not pasteurizing)

4% NEUTRAL BASE INGREDIENTS
21.5 lb. (9.75 kg) of sucrose
phosphoric acid (for pH adjustment)
700 billion cells yeast
1.3 oz. (37 g) yeast nutrients

PROCEDURES FOR SELTZER
Dilute an appropriate amount of your strong neutral base to the desired number of barrels at 4% ABV. Or brew the neutral base with the amount of sugar listed (per barrel). Add the flavoring, acid (if needed), and sugar. If you are not going to pasteurize the hard seltzer, add the potassium sorbate. Carbonate to 2.8 volumes of CO_2 if canning or to the level of CO_2 appropriate for your draught system in that case. Package (in cans or kegs) or pump to serving tanks.

PROCEDURES FOR 4% NEUTRAL BASE
If you are fermenting your neutral base at working strength, follow these instructions. Fill your mash tun with 27.0 gallons (102 L) of water (per barrel). Add the correct amount of sugar (per barrel) to your mash tun and stir until dissolved. Add water to top up to your desired volume. Check with a hydrometer or refractometer, it should read 1.032 SG or 8.0°Bx. Check the pH and adjust to an appropriate pH for your yeast, if desired. (This is around pH 5 for beer yeasts or pH 4 for wine yeasts.)

Pump the sugar slurry to your kettle and boil or hold the solution at 170°F (77°C) for 15 minutes. Cool to an appropriate temperature for your yeast strain. (For ale yeasts, cool to around 65°F, or 18°C.) Transfer the cooled sugar solution to your fermentor. (Repeat as needed to fill your fermentor.)

Aerate the mixture in the fermentor, pitch the yeast, and add yeast nutrients. Ferment in a temperature range that will produce a fast fermentation, but one that will not produce excessive esters or other yeast characters. For most neutral ale strains, 65–68°F (18–20°C) will work. Wine strains can ferment at much higher temperatures, up to 80°F (27°C). Monitor the specific gravity daily to ensure that fermentation is proceeding at a reasonable pace. If the fermentation slows beyond what it normally does early on, or the yeast is producing unusual amounts of sulfur or other by-products, a second dose of yeast nutrients may be called for. This should be ⅛–¼ the amount listed in the ingredients list. As the fermentation nears its conclusion, you may want to stir the tank gently for a few minutes per day or allow the temperature to rise slightly. Do not exceed the yeast strain's recommended working temperature range.

After fermentation, you may want to bubble CO_2 through your tanks to scrub any unwanted aromas. Likewise, you may want to either fine with activated carbon or filter your hard seltzer base through activated carbon (filtering methods are easier to work with and less messy than fining). The amount of bubbling and carbon used will depend on how clean the 4% base is. With proper yeast nutrition, fermenting a low-gravity solution such as this should not put much stress on the yeast. Once your base is brewed and cleaned up, proceed to adding the remaining ingredients as described above in the seltzer ingredients and procedures.

SLIGHTLY SWEET 5% ABV
HARD SELTZER *For 1 US barrel (31 gal., or 117 L)*

Calories per serving: 110

Flavor: grapefruit

SELTZER INGREDIENTS
31 gal. (117 L) 5.0% ABV neutral base
5.1 fl. oz. (150 mL) flavoring
citric acid (to taste)
41 oz. (1.2 kg) sucrose
0.81 oz. (23 g) potassium sorbate (necessary if not pasteurizing)

5% NEUTRAL BASE INGREDIENTS
27.0 lb. (12.3 kg) of sucrose
phosphoric acid (for pH adjustment)
880 billion cells yeast
1.4 oz. (40 g) yeast nutrients

PROCEDURES FOR SELTZER
Dilute an appropriate amount of your strong neutral base to the desired number of barrels at 5% ABV. Or brew the neutral base with the amount of sugar listed (per barrel). Add the flavoring, acid (if needed), and sugar. If you are not going to pasteurize the hard seltzer, add the potassium sorbate. Carbonate to 2.8 volumes of CO_2 if canning or to the level of CO_2 appropriate for your draught system in that case. Package (in cans or kegs) or pump to serving tanks.

PROCEDURES FOR 5% NEUTRAL BASE
If you are fermenting your neutral base at working strength, follow these instructions. Fill your mash tun with 27.0 gallons (102 L) of water (per barrel).

Add the correct amount of sugar (per barrel) to your mash tun and stir until dissolved. Add water to make your desired volume. Check the density with a hydrometer or refractometer, it should be 1.040 SG or 10°Bx. Check the pH and adjust to an appropriate pH for your yeast, if desired. (This is around pH 5 for beer yeasts or pH 4 for wine yeasts.)

Pump the sugar slurry to your kettle and boil or hold the solution at 170°F (77°C) for 15 minutes. Cool to an appropriate temperature for your yeast strain. (For ale yeasts, cool to around 65°F, or 18°C.) Transfer the cooled sugar solution to your fermentor. (Repeat as needed to fill your fermentor.)

Aerate the mixture in the fermentor, pitch the yeast, and add yeast nutrients. Ferment in a temperature range that will produce a fast fermentation, but one that will not produce excessive esters or other yeast characters. For most neutral ale strains, 65–68°F (18–20°C) will work. Wine strains can ferment at much higher temperatures, up to 80°F (27°C). Monitor the specific gravity daily to ensure that fermentation is proceeding apace. If the fermentation slows beyond what it normally does early on, or the yeast is producing unusual amounts of sulfur or other by-products, a second dose of yeast nutrients may be called for. This should be ⅛–¼ the amount listed in the ingredients list. As the fermentation nears its conclusion, you may want to stir the tank gently for a few minutes per day or allow the temperature to rise slightly. Do not exceed the yeast strain's recommended working temperature range.

After fermentation, you may want to bubble CO_2 through your tanks to scrub any unwanted aromas. Likewise, you may want to either fine with activated carbon or filter your hard seltzer base through activated carbon (filtering methods are easier to work with and less messy than fining). The amount of bubbling and carbon used will depend on how clean the 5% base is. With proper yeast nutrition, fermenting a low-gravity solution such as this should not put much stress on the yeast. Once your base is brewed and cleaned up, proceed to adding the remaining ingredients as described above in the seltzer ingredients and procedures.

EXTRA LOW CALORIE 3.5% ABV
HARD SELTZER *For 1 US barrel (31 gal., or 117 L)*

Calories per serving: 70
Flavor: pineapple

SELTZER INGREDIENTS

31 gal. (117 L) 3.5% ABV neutral base
9.3 fl. oz (275 mL) pineapple flavoring
malic acid (to taste)
12 oz. (340 g) sucrose
0.81 oz. (23 g) potassium sorbate (necessary if not pasteurizing)

3.5% NEUTRAL BASE INGREDIENTS

19.0 lb. (8.62 kg) of sucrose
phosphoric acid (for pH adjustment)
620 billion cells yeast
1.2 oz. (34 g) yeast nutrients

PROCEDURES FOR SELTZER

Dilute an appropriate amount of your strong neutral base to the desired number of barrels at 3.5% ABV. Or brew the neutral base with the amount of sugar listed (per barrel). Add the flavoring, acid (if needed), and sugar. If you are not going to pasteurize the hard seltzer, add the potassium sorbate. Carbonate to 2.8 volumes of CO_2 if canning or to the level of CO_2 appropriate for your draught system in that case. Package (in cans or kegs) or pump to serving tanks.

PROCEDURES FOR 3.5% NEUTRAL BASE

If you are fermenting your neutral base at working strength, follow these instructions. Fill your mash tun with 28.0 gallons (106 L) of water (per barrel). Add the correct amount of sugar (per barrel) to your mash tun and stir until dissolved. Add water to make your desired batch volume. Check the density with a hydrometer or refractometer, it should read 1.028 SG or 7.1°Bx. Check the pH and adjust to an appropriate pH for your yeast, if desired. (This is around pH 5 for beer yeasts or pH 4 for wine yeasts.)

Pump the sugar slurry to your kettle and boil or hold the solution at 170°F (77°C) for 15 minutes. Cool to an appropriate temperature for your yeast strain. (For ale yeasts, cool to around 65°F, or 18°C.) Transfer the cooled sugar solution to your fermentor. (Repeat as needed to fill your fermentor.)

Aerate the mixture in the fermentor, pitch the yeast, and add yeast nutrients. Ferment in a temperature range that will produce a fast fermentation, but one that will not produce excessive esters or other yeast characters. For most neutral ale strains, 65–68°F (18–20°C) will work. Wine strains can ferment at much higher temperatures, up to 80°F (27°C). Monitor the specific gravity daily to ensure that fermentation is proceeding apace. If the fermentation slows beyond what it normally does early on, or the yeast is producing unusual amounts of sulfur or other by-products, a second dose of yeast nutrients may be called for. This should be ⅛–¼ the amount listed in the ingredients list. As the fermentation nears its conclusion, you may want to stir the tank gently for a few minutes per day or allow the temperature to rise slightly. Do not exceed the yeast strain's recommended working temperature range.

After fermentation, you may want to bubble CO_2 through your tanks to scrub any unwanted aromas. Likewise, you may want to either fine with activated carbon or filter your hard seltzer base through activated carbon. The amount of bubbling and carbon used will depend on how clean the 3.5% base is. With proper yeast nutrition, fermenting a low-gravity solution such as this should not put much stress on the yeast. Once your base is brewed and cleaned up, proceed to adding the remaining ingredients as described above in the seltzer ingredients and procedures.

SLIGHTLY STRONGER 6% ABV
HARD SELTZER *For 1 US barrel (31 gal., or 117 L)*

Calories per serving: 115
Flavor: orange

SELTZER INGREDIENTS
31 gal. (117 L) 6.0% ABV neutral base
9.3 fl. oz. (275 mL) orange flavoring
citric acid (to taste)
12 oz. (340 g) sucrose
0.81 oz. (23 g) potassium sorbate

6.0% NEUTRAL BASE INGREDIENTS
32.0 lb. (14.5 kg) sucrose
phosphoric acid (for pH adjustment)
1,023 billion cells yeast
1.5 oz. (43 g) yeast nutrients

PROCEDURES FOR SELTZER

Dilute an appropriate amount of your strong neutral base to the desired number of barrels at 6% ABV. Or brew the neutral base with the amount of sugar listed (per barrel). Add the flavoring, acid (if needed), and sugar. If you are not going to pasteurize the hard seltzer, add the potassium sorbate. Carbonate to 2.8 volumes of CO_2 if canning or to the level of CO_2 appropriate for your draught system in that case. Package (in cans or kegs) or pump to serving tanks.

PROCEDURES FOR 6% NEUTRAL BASE

If you are fermenting your neutral base at working strength, follow these instructions. Fill your mash tun with 27.0 gallons (102 L) of water (per barrel). Add the correct amount of sugar (per barrel) to your mash tun and stir until dissolved. Add water to make your desired batch size. Check the density with a hydrometer or refractometer, the reading should be 1.047 SG or 11.7°Bx. Check the pH and adjust to an appropriate pH for your yeast, if desired. (This is around pH 5 for beer yeasts or pH 4 for wine yeasts.)

Pump the sugar slurry to your kettle and boil or hold the solution at 170°F (77°C) for 15 minutes. Cool to an appropriate temperature for your yeast strain. (For ale yeasts, cool to around 65°F, or 18°C.) Transfer the cooled sugar solution to your fermentor. (Repeat as needed to fill your fermentor.)

Aerate the mixture, pitch the yeast, and add yeast nutrients. Ferment in a temperature range that will produce a fast fermentation, but one that will not produce excessive esters or other yeast characters. For most neutral ale strains, 65–68°F (18–20°C) will work. Wine strains can ferment at much higher temperatures, up to 80°F (27°C). Monitor the specific gravity daily to ensure that fermentation is proceeding apace. If the fermentation slows beyond what it normally does early on, or the yeast is producing unusual amounts of sulfur or other by-products, a second dose of yeast nutrients may be called for. This should be ⅛–¼ the amount listed in the ingredients list. As the fermentation nears its conclusion, you may want to stir the tank gently for a few minutes per day or allow the temperature to rise slightly. Do not exceed the yeast strain's recommended working temperature range.

After fermentation, you may want to bubble CO_2 through your tanks to scrub any unwanted aromas. Likewise, you may want to either fine with activated carbon or filter your hard seltzer base through activated carbon (filtering methods are easier to work with and less messy than fining). The amount of bubbling and carbon used will depend on how clean the 6% base is. With proper yeast nutrition, fermenting a low-gravity solution such as this should not put much stress on the yeast. Once your base is brewed and cleaned up, proceed to adding the remaining ingredients as described above in the seltzer ingredients and procedures.

MODERATELY STRONG 7% ABV
HARD SELTZER *For 1 US barrel (31 gal., or 117 L)*

Calories per serving: 135
Flavor: lemon

INGREDIENTS
31 gal. (117 L) 7% ABV neutral base
6.3 fl. oz. (185 mL) lemon flavoring
citric acid (to taste)
18 oz. (500 g) sucrose
0.81 oz. (23 g) potassium sorbate

7.0% NEUTRAL BASE INGREDIENTS
37.5 lb. (17.0 kg) sucrose
phosphoric acid (for pH adjustment)
1,200 billion cells yeast
1.6 oz. (45 g) yeast nutrients

SELTZER PROCEDURES
Dilute an appropriate amount of your strong neutral base to the desired number of barrels at 7.0% ABV. Or brew the neutral base with the amount of sugar listed (per barrel). Add the flavoring, acid (if needed), and sugar. If you are not going to pasteurize the hard seltzer, add the potassium sorbate. Carbonate to 2.8 volumes of CO_2 if canning or the level of CO_2 appropriate for your draught system in that case. Package (in cans or kegs) or pump to serving tanks.

PROCEDURES FOR 7% NEUTRAL BASE
If you are fermenting your neutral base at working strength, follow these instructions. Fill your mash tun with 26.5 gallons (100 L) of water (per barrel). Add the correct amount of sugar (per barrel) to your mash tun and stir until dissolved. Add water to reach your batch size. Check the density with a hydrometer or refractometer, it should be 1.056 SG or 13.8°Bx. Check the pH and adjust to an appropriate pH for your yeast, if desired. (This is around pH 5 for beer yeasts or pH 4 for wine yeasts.)

Pump the sugar slurry to your kettle and boil or hold the solution at 170°F (77°C) for 15 minutes. Cool to an appropriate temperature for your yeast strain. (For ale yeasts, cool to around 65°F, or 18°C.) Transfer the cooled sugar solution to your fermentor. (Repeat as needed to fill your fermentor.)

Aerate the mixture in the fermentor, pitch the yeast, and add yeast nutrients. Ferment in a temperature range that will produce a fast fermentation, but one that will not produce excessive esters or other yeast characters. For most neutral ale strains, 65–68°F (18–20°C) will work. Wine strains can ferment at much higher temperatures, up to 80°F (27°C). Monitor the specific gravity daily to ensure that fermentation is proceeding apace. If the fermentation slows beyond what it normally does early on, or the yeast is producing unusual amounts of sulfur or other by-products, a second dose of yeast nutrients may be called for. This should be ⅛–¼ the amount listed in the ingredients list. As the fermentation nears its conclusion, you may want to stir the tank gently for a few minutes per day or allow the temperature to rise slightly. Do not exceed the yeast strain's recommended working temperature range.

After fermentation, you may want to bubble CO_2 through your tanks to scrub any unwanted aromas. Likewise, you may want to either fine with activated carbon or filter your hard seltzer base through activated carbon (filtering methods are easier to work with and less messy than fining). The amount of bubbling and carbon used will depend on how clean the 7% base is. With proper yeast nutrition, fermenting a low-gravity solution such as this should not put much stress on the yeast. Once your base is brewed and cleaned up, proceed to adding the remaining ingredients as described above in the seltzer ingredients and procedures.

STRONG 8% ABV
HARD SELTZER *For 1 US barrel (31 gal., or 117 L)*

Calories per serving: 155
Flavor: blueberry

SELTZER INGREDIENTS
31 gal. (117 L) 8% ABV neutral base
30.4 fl. oz. (900 mL) flavoring
malic acid (to taste)
23 oz. (650 g) sucrose
0.81 oz. (23 g) potassium sorbate

8.0% NEUTRAL BASE INGREDIENTS
42.5 b. (19.3 kg) sucrose
phosphoric acid (for pH adjustment)
1,400 billion cells yeast
1.7 oz. (48 g) yeast nutrients

PROCEDURES FOR SELTZER
Dilute an appropriate amount of your strong neutral base to the desired number of barrels at 8.0% ABV. Or brew the neutral base with the amount of sugar listed (per barrel). Add the flavoring, acid (if needed), and sugar. If you are not going to pasteurize the hard seltzer, add the potassium sorbate. Carbonate to 2.8 volumes of CO_2 if canning or to the level of CO_2 appropriate for your draught system in that case. Package (in cans or kegs) or pump to serving tanks.

PROCEDURES FOR 8% NEUTRAL BASE
If you are fermenting your neutral base at working strength, follow these instructions. Fill your mash tun with 26 gallons (98 L) of water (per barrel). Add the correct amount of sugar (per barrel) to your mash tun and stir until dissolved. Add water to top up to correct batch size. Check the density with a hydrometer or refractometer, it should read 1.063 SG or 15.4°Bx. Check the pH and adjust to an appropriate pH for your yeast, if desired. Pump the sugar slurry to your kettle and boil for 15 minutes. Cool to an appropriate temperature for your yeast strain. (For ale yeasts, cool to around 65°F, or 18°C.) Transfer the cooled sugar solution to your fermentor. (Repeat as needed to fill your fermentor.)

Aerate the mixture in the fermentor, pitch the yeast, and add yeast nutrients. Ferment in a temperature range that will produce a fast fermentation, but one that will not produce excessive esters or other yeast characters. For most neutral ale strains, 65–68°F (18–20°C) will work. Wine strains can ferment at much higher temperatures, up to 80°F (27°C). Monitor the specific gravity daily to ensure that fermentation is proceeding apace. If the fermentation slows beyond what it normally does early on, or the yeast is producing unusual amounts of sulfur or other by-products, a second dose of yeast nutrients may be called for. This should be ⅛–¼ the amount listed in the ingredients list. As the fermentation nears its conclusion, you may want to stir the tank gently for a few minutes per day or allow the temperature to rise slightly. Do not exceed the yeast strain's recommended working temperature range.

After fermentation, you may want to bubble CO_2 through your tanks to scrub any unwanted aromas. Likewise, you may want to either fine with activated carbon or filter your hard seltzer base through activated carbon (filtering methods are easier to work with and less messy than fining). The amount of bubbling and carbon used will depend on how clean the 8% base is. With proper yeast nutrition, fermentation should not put much stress on the yeast. Once your base is brewed and cleaned up, proceed to adding the remaining ingredients as described above in the seltzer ingredients and procedures.

NEUTRAL BASE RECIPES

10% ABV NEUTRAL BASE *For 1 US barrel (31 gal., or 117 L)*

When diluted 1:1 with de-aerated water, this neutral base can be used to generate twice its volume of 5% ABV hard seltzer.

INGREDIENTS
53 lb. (24 kg) sucrose
1,800 billion cells yeast
1.8 oz. (51 g) complete yeast nutrients

PROCEDURES
Fill your kettle with 26 gallons (98 L) of water (per barrel). Add the correct amount of sucrose (per barrel) and stir to dissolve. Top up to your full volume. The resulting specific gravity should be 1.079 or 19°Bx. Boil or hold the solution at 170°F (77°C) for 15 minutes. Cool to an appropriate temperature for your yeast strain and transfer the cooled sugar solution to your fermentor. (Repeat as needed to fill your fermentor.)

Aerate the mixture in the fermentor, pitch the yeast, and add the yeast nutrients. Ferment in a temperature range that will produce a fast fermentation, but one that will not produce excessive esters or other yeast characters. Monitor the fermentation temperature and keep it in line with your yeast strain's recommended temperature. Also keep track of the density of the solution to see that the fermentation is proceeding at a reasonable pace.

Near the end of fermentation, rousing the tank and allowing the temperature to rise a bit may help the yeast finish. Assess the neutral base and determine if you need to scrub any flavor or aromas. Bubbling CO_2 through the solution will scrub aromas. Filtering through or fining with activated carbon will remove flavors, aromas, and color.

12% ABV NEUTRAL BASE *For 1 US barrel (31 gal., or 117 L)*

When diluted 2:1 with de-aerated water, this neutral base can be used to generate three times its volume of 4% ABV hard seltzer.

INGREDIENTS
63.5 lb. (28.8 kg) sucrose
1,800 billion cells yeast
2.0 oz. (57 g) complete yeast nutrients

PROCEDURES
Fill your kettle with 25 gallons (95 L) of water (per barrel). Add the correct amount of sucrose (per barrel) and stir to dissolve. Top up to your full volume. The resulting specific gravity should be 1.094 or 22°Bx. Boil or hold the solution at 170°F (77°C) for 15 minutes. Cool to an appropriate temperature for your yeast strain and transfer the cooled sugar solution to your fermentor. (Repeat as needed to fill your fermentor.)

Aerate the mixture in the fermentor, pitch the yeast, and add the yeast nutrients. Ferment in a temperature range that will produce a fast fermentation, but one that will not produce excessive esters or other yeast characters. Monitor the fermentation temperature and keep it in line with your yeast strain's recommended temperature. Also keep track of the density of the solution to see that the fermentation is proceeding at a reasonable pace.

Near the end of fermentation, rousing the tank and allowing the temperature to rise a bit may help the yeast finish. Assess the neutral base and determine if you need to scrub any flavor or aromas. Bubbling CO_2 through the solution will scrub aromas. Filtering through or fining with activated carbon will remove flavors, aromas, and color.

GOVERNMENT REGULATIONS

COMMERCIAL BEER PRODUCTION IN THE US is regulated by the Alcohol and Tobacco Tax and Trade Bureau (TTB). The TTB is a bureau of the United States Department of the Treasury. It was formed in 2003 when the law enforcement functions of the Bureau of Alcohol, Tobacco and Firearms (ATF) were transferred to the Department of Justice. The responsibilities for taxation and trade regulation remained with the Department of the Treasury, to be handled by the newly created TBB.

This chapter gives an overview of TTB and other federal regulations that are applicable to hard seltzers. It is expected that brewers will already be familiar with the regulations that apply to "normal" beer and brewery operations. For guidance, the resource hub at the Brewers Association website can help:

- https://www.brewersassociation.org/resource-hub/ttb/

TTB regulations can seem labyrinthine at first glance. However, their webpage can help guide you through the process:

- https://www.ttb.gov/alcohol/beverage-alcohol

Commercial brewers should familiarize themselves with the relevant regulations for hard seltzer production and be aware that they can change over time. In addition, specific state regulations—which are not comprehensively covered here—may also apply. Brewers operating outside of the United States will have that country's own set of regulations to follow.

BEER AND MALT BEVERAGES

The TTB regulates ingredients, processes, labeling, and advertising of beer and malt beverages. Brewed hard seltzers may be categorized as either beers or malt beverages and thus fall under the TTB's jurisdiction. Brewed hard seltzers may contain added alcohol, however, including alcohol that may be contained in the added flavorings. For any type of brewed hard seltzer—either beer or flavored malt beverage—that is under 6% ABV, up to 49% of the ethanol in the beverage can come from distilled alcohol, whether part of the flavor extract or not. If the beverage is close to the maximum amount of added alcohol allowed under the 49% rule, the brewer may want to apply for a drawback (credit) or else they will actually be paying taxes on the alcohol present in the flavoring at the time the flavoring is purchased and also when the final beverage is sold. If the hard seltzer is stronger than 6% ABV, the amount of added alcohol is limited to 1.5%.

BEER

Beer is defined by the Internal Revenue Code (IRC) of 1986 as

> beer, ale, porter, stout, and other similar fermented beverages (including sake or similar products) of any name or description containing one-half of 1 percent or more of alcohol by volume, brewed or produced from malt, wholly or in part, or from any substitute therefor. (26 U.S.C. § 5052(a))

The IRC is enforced by the Internal Revenue Service, which is, of course, a bureau of the Department of the Treasury.

The TTB definition of beer, found in 27 C.F.R. 25.11, is essentially the same as that in the IRC. However, the TTB regulations further stipulate what qualifies as a malt substitute (27 C.F.R. 25.15(a)): "Only rice, grain of any kind, bran, glucose, sugar, and molasses are substitutes for malt."

MALT BEVERAGES

A malt beverage must contain malt and hops, although it can contain other ingredients. The Federal Alcohol Administration (FAA) is an agency of the Department of the Treasury, formed in 1935 to regulate alcohol after the repeal of Prohibition. Here is how a malt beverage is defined in the FAA Act:

> [A] beverage made by the alcoholic fermentation of an infusion or decoction, or combination of both, in potable brewing water, of malted barley with hops, or their parts, or their products, and with or without other malted cereals, and with or without the addition of unmalted or prepared cereals, other carbohydrates or products prepared therefrom, and with or without the addition of carbon dioxide, and with or without other wholesome products suitable for human food consumption. (27 U.S.C. § 211(a)(7))

The same definition appears in the TTB regulations at 27 C.F.R. 7.10.

BEER VERSUS MALT BEVERAGES

The key difference between beer and malt beverages is that beer—by the TTB definition—does not need to contain malted barley or hops. In addition, a minimum alcohol content of 0.5% ABV is specified for beer but not for malt beverages. Thus, a hard seltzer made from fermenting a sugar solution and adding a flavoring qualifies as a beer under these regulations. To qualify as a malt beverage, some malted barley and hops would have to be used. (Specifically, 25% malted barley and 7.5 lb. of hops per 100 bbl.) Another difference is that a malt beverage (brewed with malt and hops) does not require FDA labeling but a beer brewed from just sugar does.

These definitions are the opposite of what many brewers might think before familiarizing themselves with the regulations. Brewers tend to think of beer as a beverage containing malt and hops, whereas malt beverages—especially a flavored malt beverage (FMB)—are considered as something similar to beer but not really beer. Under the TTB definitions, a "regular" IPA would be considered a malt beverage but a drink like hard seltzer made from fermenting just sugar is a beer. For this reason, some brewers refer to beers under this definition as "IRC beers."

The TTB ruling 2008-3 details the relevant distinctions between beer and malted beverages in the context of the IRC of 1986 and the FAA Act.

Additional discussion can be found in TTB ruling 2015-1. Both rulings can be accessed from the TTB website:

- https://www.ttb.gov/images/pdfs/rulings/2008-3.pdf
- https://www.ttb.gov/images/pdfs/rulings/ttb-ruling-2015-1-malt-beverage-formulas.pdf

The significance of these definitions is that the Internal Revenue Service classifies a beverage brewed by fermenting sugar as a beer and taxes it as such. Thus, a hard seltzer made from fermenting sugar will be taxed at a lower rate than one made by adding distilled spirits to carbonated water.

APPROVALS REQUIRED

To brew a hard seltzer you will need a Brewers Notice, as you would for brewing any beer. In addition, TTB formula approval is required for most hard seltzers. The usual TTB label approval (COLA) is not needed for most hard seltzers, but breweries must abide by FDA guidelines.

FORMULA APPROVAL

Almost all hard seltzers require formula approval. You can check if yours does by using the following interactive page on the TTB's website. Just answer a few questions and it will tell you if you need formula approval.

- https://www.ttb.gov/formulation/which-alcohol-beverages-require-formula-approval-beer-and-malt-beverages-mb

Typical brewed beverages produced in a commercial brewery, that is, beer in the usual sense of the word, do not require formula approval. By contrast, most hard seltzers do. This is largely because brewed beverages using non-traditional techniques (such as processes used to remove color and flavor) or additional flavoring and coloring agents require TTB formula approval.

Using activated carbon to strip color and flavor from a hard seltzer is considered a non-traditional procedure. Formula approval also proves that a beverage does not contain any prohibited ingredients (or limited ingredients). Ingredients that are categorized as generally recognized as safe (GRAS) by the FDA can be used in hard seltzers. Further guidance can be found at:

- https://www.ttb.gov/formulation/determining-if-and-how-ingredients-may-be-used-in-your-beverage

TTB limited ingredients, and the amounts in which they can be used, can be found at:

- https://www.ttb.gov/scientific-services-division/limited-ingredients

The normal ingredients for brewing beer, including many ingredients used for brewing specialty beers, may be used without seeking formula approval. The addition of flavorings or coloring requires formula approval and you will need to get a TTB/ATF number for each flavoring used. Manufacturers of flavors used in hard seltzers are aware of this and will have all the information you need, including the alcohol percentage in the flavoring, which can be found on the flavor ingredient data sheet (FIDS).

The entire process of formula approval can be done online by going to the TTB's "Alcohol Beverage Formula Approval" webpage:

- https://www.ttb.gov/formulation/

If you need help, you can download the "Formulas Online 2.0 Online Industry Member User Manual" at:

- https://www.ttb.gov/images/pdfs/foia_fonl-docs/fonl_oim_um.pdf.

This 295-page user manual will guide you step by step through the process. You need to have a Brewer's Notice to submit a formula for approval. You also need to apply for an online account to use the online formula application process. This same account allows you to use the online COLA application process, should you have beverages requiring this (see below).

WHEN LABEL APPROVAL (COLA) IS NEEDED

For most 'ordinary' beers (or malt beverages, using the TTB's definition above), you also need to get a Certificate of Label Approval (COLA) for the label. As with formula approval, this can all be done online:

- https://www.ttb.gov/labeling/colas

The online manual, entitled "COLAs Online 3.11.3 Public COLA Registry User Manual," will guide you through the process and is only 50 pages long. Within the user manual are links to the proper forms, available to submit electronically or as printable forms that can be mailed in. You will need to get formula approval—assuming your malt beverage needs it—before applying for a COLA.

The labeling of hard seltzers made only from sugar (i.e., IRC beers) is governed by FDA regulations and therefore a COLA is not required. However, the FDA requires a number of things on labels.

FDA LABELING

Any beer brewed without malted barley and hops (i.e., an IRC beer) requires FDA-compliant labeling. The FDA has an online document, "Labeling of Certain Beers Subject to the Labeling Jurisdiction of the Food and Drug Administration:

Guidance for Industry," which details the process and can be found at:

- https://www.fda.gov/regulatory-information/search-fda-guidance
  -documents/guidance-industry-labeling-certain-beers-subject
  -labeling-jurisdiction-food-and-drug-administration

This guidance document addresses the changes brought about by TTB Ruling 2008-3, in which sugar became a substitute for malt. Further information on labeling can be found at:

- https://www.fda.gov/regulatory-information/search-fda-guidance
  -documents/guidance-industry-food-labeling-guide

You do not submit paperwork to the FDA to get label approval. The FDA will audit you if it receives consumer complaints or believes you have not met the requirements.

The highlights of these FDA documents are easy to summarize. A label must include a statement of identity. This tells the consumer what the product is. For a hard seltzer, "beer (or alcoholic beverage) brewed from sugar," or any reasonable, accurate variant will suffice.

The net quantity of the contents must be given, preferably in both US customary units and metric units, although only US customary units are required. As you might expect, these measurements need to be accurate. The statement of identity and net quantity must appear on the front label, which is the principle display panel (PDP). The name and place of business of the producer must also be given.

Water is the most abundant ingredient in a hard seltzer. If a brewer wants to describe their water as filtered or purified, they should review FDA guidelines (under 21 C.F.R. 165.110). These standards are tightly regulated due to the bottled water industry.

A major part of meeting FDA requirements for any label is the nutrition panel. This includes a statement of ingredients listed in descending order of predominance by weight. Any added flavors or colors must be included in this list. Ingredients should be GRAS or, for limited ingredients, used in amounts that are allowed. (Most limited ingredients are coloring agents and one option to avoid any problems caused by their inclusion would be not to use them or products that contain them.) The panel should also include nutritional information, although this requirement can be waived for small businesses. Each element of the nutrition panel has requirements, such as typeface and type size, which are outlined in the FDA documents cited above.

Major food allergens, including peanuts, shellfish, and wheat, must be declared if they are present. If your brewery is certified as making a gluten-free product, this information is allowed on the label. Only IRC beers can be declared gluten-free. Malt beverages cannot. However, in general, the brewer should not make any health claims on the label—and be aware that the FDA takes a broad view of health claims. Likewise, you can declare your hard seltzer GMO-free if it does not contain any genetically modified organisms. In this regard, sugar, the second most abundant ingredient in a hard seltzer, is not considered a GMO ingredient. This is the case for glucose/dextrose (corn sugar), even if the corn it was extracted from was GMO—the rationale is that no DNA from the corn exists in the sugar. The brewer can leave "corn sugar" off the label and instead list the ingredient as alcohol, because the sugar is converted into alcohol. (This also allows the brewer to switch from corn sugar to cane sugar without changing the label.)

Acids are also a major component in some hard seltzers. All the major food use acidulants, including citric acid, are considered GRAS by the FDA. Note that citric acid is a component of many citrus fruits and may be added in that manner as opposed to a purified compound.

The label may contain the name of a cocktail, unless that name contains the name of another company or brand.

In the past, the brewing industry was reluctant to put nutritional information on their product labels. It was thought that the caloric content (and possibly other aspects) would dissuade consumers from purchasing beer. But for hard seltzers the caloric content, low amount of carbohydrates, and lack of gluten (where applicable) are major selling points.

CANADIAN AND US STATE REGULATIONS

Your hard seltzer will need to meet the requirements of whatever country or US state it is sold in. Canada's regulations can be found at:

- https://www.canada.ca/en/health-canada/services/food-nutrition /legislation-guidelines/guidance-documents/flavoured-purified -alcohol.html

Be aware that some US states require hops to be in any product classified (and taxed) as a beer. Until recently, Florida defined both beer and malt beverages to mean that all brewed beverages must be made with at least some malt (hops were not mentioned), but this requirement was done away with after lobbying from the industry. There are other state-specific requirements that brewers should watch out for. Oregon, for example, treats hard seltzers as a wine and requires a winery license to produce them.

THE PRESENT AND THE FUTURE

A change in the wording of how beer was defined by the Internal Revenue Code—rendering sugar as a malt substitute—paved the way for the brewing of hard seltzers. The trend of valuing low-calorie beverages, with other perceived health benefits, caused consumers to embrace these beverages and make them staggeringly popular. However, some in the industry worry about possible changes to beverage regulations in the future that this surge in popularity may engender. Specifically, now that brewed beverages that taste like seltzer water with added alcohol are available, will the government re-evaluate the tax structure on alcoholic beverages; will beer still be afforded the tax break compared to packaged mixed drinks when it essentially mimics them? Even if nothing comes of this, brewers of hard seltzers should keep track of any potential changes in regulation. Any new, booming business is likely to attract some attention from regulators and brewers should be ready for change.

© Brewers Association/Luke Trautwein

7

MAKING
HARD SELTZER AT HOME

IF YOU ARE A HOME brewer, winemaker, or mead maker, you may want to try your hand at making hard seltzer or something similar. There are some technical challenges to making a hard seltzer at home, but they are not insurmountable. Any experienced homebrewer can make a satisfactory hard seltzer using only ordinary homebrewing equipment. If you are interested in making a hard seltzer up to commercial standards, you will need to get a suitable activated carbon filter. However, there are some workarounds that can achieve higher clarity without filtration.

If you have never fermented beer or wine at home before, or you have no interest in doing so, you can make hard seltzer with the bare minimum of equipment. Appendix A at the end of this book will talk you through the basics of making your own hard seltzer and does not assume any prior brewing experience.

EQUIPMENT

Any "regular" homebrewing setup—even the simplest—should allow you to make a hard seltzer at home. At a minimum, you will need the pieces discussed in this section.

In the US, most homebrewing setups are designed around producing 5.0 gallons (19 L) of beer at a time. So, this equipment list will assume you are making the same amount of hard seltzer. It is possible to make more or less, of course. The adjustments required for this should be obvious, mostly involving a larger or smaller kettle and an appropriately sized fermentor.

For a five-gallon (19 L) batch of hard seltzer, you should have a stainless steel pot that is at least five gallons in volume to use as your kettle. Seven to ten gallons (27–38 L) would be better, because with this size kettle you can boil a little over five gallons of sugar wash (the unfermented hard seltzer base mixture) down to five gallons. While a five-gallon pot would also work, you would need to boil about 4.25 gal. (16 L) down to a bit over 4.0 gal. (15 L), then dilute the mixture to 5.0 gal. (19 L) in your fermentor. If you attempt to boil a higher-gravity wash for a five-gallon batch at a volume smaller than four gallons, you run the risk of scorching sugar to the bottom of the pot.

After the boil, you will need a way to cool your sugar wash. This can be done in a large sink or bathtub with some ice water, but a wort chiller is a much better choice. A long, sturdy spoon for stirring will also come in handy.

You need a 6.0–7.0 gal. (23–27 L) primary fermentor to ferment a five-gallon batch of hard seltzer. The fermentor can be a bucket, carboy, or stainless steel cylindroconical fermentor. For a variety of reasons that will become clear later, one reason being that additions will need to be made during fermentation, a bucket fermentor is an excellent choice. A five-gallon (19 L) carboy to use as a secondary fermentor is very helpful, although not strictly necessary. You will also need a way to transfer the chilled wash from the kettle to the fermentor and, later, the fermented hard seltzer from the fermentor to the packaging. If your kettle and your fermentors have a spigot, all you need is some food-grade plastic tubing (Tygon tubing). If not, you will need a racking cane. A siphon starter can be handy but is not required. Your fermentor will need a fermentation lock (also called an airlock) and a drilled stopper to attach the fermentation lock to the fermentor.

Once the hard seltzer has fermented and cleared, you will need one or more vessels in which to package the hard seltzer. A five-gallon (19 L) Cornelius ("corny") keg is the best option. With a keg, you can force carbonate the beverage and serve it without worrying about the yeast sediment that settles to the bottom of bottle-conditioned beverages.

Bottle conditioning is an option if you are not bothered by a little bit of yeast sediment at the bottom of every bottle. You will need fifty-four 12 fl. oz. (355 mL) bottles to package 5.0 gal. (19 L) of hard seltzer; alternatively, you can use twenty-nine 22 fl. oz. (650 mL) bottles. You will also need a bottling bucket in which to mix the hard seltzer and the priming sugar. Finally, obviously, you need a bottle capper and the appropriate number of uncrimped crown bottle caps.

MAKING A HARD SELTZER

The basic idea behind brewing a hard seltzer is simple: you mix a sugar wash, ferment it, then flavor and carbonate it. A *sugar wash* is simply the name for an unfermented mixture of simple sugar and water. The term is the equivalent of *wort* in brewing or *must* in wine making.

All your brewing equipment must be clean before you start. Your fermentor—in fact, any surface that the sugar wash will touch after chilling—should be sanitized. Visually inspect everything, especially surfaces that will be in contact with chilled sugar wash. If you see even the smallest amount of soil, clean it again.

In many cases, especially when using liquid yeast, you will want to make a yeast starter two or three days ahead of time in order for your pitching rate to be adequate. If you are using dried yeast, you can simply add the proper amount of yeast when pitching. If your hard seltzer recipe does not specify a pitching rate, assume the pitching rate is either the normal ale pitching rate—1.0 million cells per milliliter per degree Plato—or up to 50% higher. For a 5.0 gal. (19 L) batch of 4.0%–5.0% ABV hard seltzer, this amounts to roughly 150–270 billion cells.

Not all homebrewers have the equipment to count yeast cells. However, if you make a 2.0–3.0 qt. (1.9–2.8 L) yeast starter with a starter solution (wash, wort, or must) at around 1.020 specific gravity (SG), you should end up with approximately the right number of cells when the starter has fermented. The ingredients for your starter solution can be sugar, malt extract (or wort), grape juice, or a mixture of these. The color in the yeast starter should be as light as possible as some of the liquid will end up being transferred to the main batch along with the yeast. You should add a small amount of yeast nutrients regardless of the starter solution used. As with any fermentation, pay extra attention to the cleaning and sanitation of your yeast starter vessel. Any small amount of contamination in the starter will be amplified in the main fermentation.

If you are using brewer's yeast, a starter made with roughly equal amounts of the lightest malt extract you can find and sugar is a good option. For a 5.0 gal. (19 L) batch, the volume of the starter should be 2.0–3.0 qt. (1.9–2.8 L). Make the starter solution so it has a specific gravity of around 1.020, which, for the volume range given, should take 2.0–3.0 oz. (57–85 g) each of dried malt extract and sucrose (table sugar). Add just a gram or two ("a pinch") of complete yeast nutrients. Bring the solution to a boil and simmer for a few minutes. All you need to do is sanitize the solution. Sprinkle the yeast nutrients into the mix once it comes to a boil. (Keep in mind that if you use malt extract, which is made from barley, to raise your yeast starter, it may result in trace amounts of gluten being present in your hard seltzer.)

If your starter vessel is made of borosilicate glass or stainless steel, carefully pour the hot starter solution into the vessel. Cap with aluminum foil (or close the lid) and cool the vessel. If your starter vessel is ordinary flint glass, cool the starter solution and then pour it into the starter vessel. When you are certain the starter solution is at the right temperature, aerate it. In this instance, the right temperature is any temperature at which the yeast can function properly. This depends on the yeast strain. You can aerate by vigorously shaking the vessel, assuming you can keep it from leaking as you do so. You can also use a sintered aeration stone and aerate with HEPA-filtered air or oxygen.

Next, pitch the yeast to your starter as quickly as is feasible. The oxygen dissolved in the starter solution will be diffusing out of solution, assuming you aerated the starter above the volume of gas it would normally hold at atmospheric pressure. This does not happen instantly, so you do not need to rush, just avoid taking your lunch break between aerating and pitching the yeast. Depending on how the yeast is packaged, you may want to wipe down the outside of the yeast package with sanitizing solution before opening it. Then, pour or sprinkle the yeast and swirl the starter. Set the starter somewhere at "room temperature" or slightly above and shield it from strong light. It should ferment to completion in 2–3 days. Depending on the type of yeast, all or most of the yeast may flocculate and form a dense layer at the bottom of the starter.

If you are using wine yeast, your starter could be made from very light, white grape juice and sucrose. As with the malt extract starter, aim for around 1.020 SG and include a pinch of yeast nutrients. You will only need 2.0–2.5 qt. (1.9–2.4 L) of grape juice starter for a 5 gal. (19 L) batch fermented with wine yeast. You can very lightly simmer the starter, cool as described above, and pitch the yeast. Or you can skip heating the mixture and add a tiny amount of potassium metabisulfite powder and pitch the yeast the next day.

Distiller's yeast is yet another option. The starter volume and specific gravity will be very similar to that for brewer's or wine yeast. Make the starter from sucrose (or glucose) and let it ferment somewhere warm. Some distiller's yeast is packaged with its own yeast nutrients built in. Some of these nutrients will be used up when the starter ferments, so you may want to add a pinch of yeast nutrients to the main batch to make up for this. Do not overdo it on yeast nutrients though—more is not better.

MAKING THE SUGAR WASH

The first step on brew day is to make your sugar wash. This is the sugar solution that the yeast will ferment to make alcohol. This is typically fermented without the flavor addition, including any acid added for flavor. The fermented sugar wash is the "neutral" base beverage to which you add flavor, acidity, and carbonation.

Making the sugar wash is extremely straightforward. Some commercial breweries make a (relatively) high-gravity sugar wash and dilute it to near working strength after fermentation. For homebrewers, it is easier to make the sugar wash at working strength. High-gravity fermentations stress the yeast more and you want the lowest level of yeast by-products, such as esters, that you can manage. Diluting a high-gravity beverage to working strength is also best done with de-aerated water, and this requires boiling the dilution water, then quickly cooling it. It is not impossible to do at home but unless you are trying to brew a lot of hard seltzer, or wish to emulate how some commercial brewers do it, simply making a working strength sugar wash is a lot easier.

As with any brew day, it is best to assemble all your equipment before you start. Make sure that it is cleaned and, if needed, sanitized. It will be helpful if you write out a checklist of the major steps. Then, as you brew, you can check them off the list.

The fermented sugar wash is meant to be neutral—a flavorless canvas for which to add flavor and perhaps color. As such, the water you use must meet all the usual requirements for brewing. And you should really assess the taste of the water alone before using it. If your tap water has any detectable off-flavor or aroma, you either need to carbon filter it until it tastes clean or find another source of water.

Municipal water supplies are usually treated with some form of chlorine compound for sanitation. To remove this chlorine, most homebrewers either filter their water through a carbon filter or treat it with potassium metabisulfite. The latter can be done by adding one standard Campden tablet per 20 gal. (76 L) of water to be treated.

Your kettle should be able to hold the entire volume you plan to boil (see below) and about 20% extra. Begin heating your water. Add small amounts of sugar as the water heats, stirring frequently so none sinks to the bottom and scorches. Do not pour in all of the sugar called for at once. Break it into smaller aliquots and add them gradually. The sugar can be dextrose (glucose), sucrose, or any other simple sugar including, for example, candi sugar, agave syrup, rice syrup solids, or Brewers Crystals. Of these, dextrose or sucrose will give the most neutral base. For 5.0 gal. (19 L) of sugar wash, you will need 3.3–4.3 lb. (1.5–2.0 kg) of sucrose or 4.2–5.2 lb. (1.9–2.4 kg) of glucose (monohydrate), also called corn sugar. The specific gravity should be 1.031 to 1.038 to yield a finished base around 4.0%–5.0% ABV. The actual ABV will depend both on the starting gravity after the boil and the final gravity of the solution after fermentation.

If you are boiling the full volume of sugar wash, your starting volume should be 5.25 gal. (19.9 L). This should yield 5.0 gal. (19 L) of sugar wash at the specified specific gravity after a 15-minute boil. Before the boil, the specific gravity will be slightly less because the volume is greater than five gallons. Also, if the hydrometer sample is warm your specific gravity reading will be lower than the true specific gravity. Make sure to take hydrometer readings at the temperature your hydrometer is calibrated to, which is usually listed right on the device. A refractometer can also be used to measure the density of the solution before yeast is pitched.

If you like, you can boil a sugar wash that is thicker than required and dilute to your intended strength in the fermentor. (This is how most malt extract worts are made.) This may be an option if your kettle is too small for a full-volume boil or if you are trying to get the most hard seltzer possible from a single kettle boil. However, if you have the ability to boil (and cool) your full volume, it is probably best to do that. That way you lower the chances of darkening the wash during the boil and do not have to worry about preparing dilution water.

If you are boiling less than the full amount and diluting it to five gallons (19 L) in the fermentor, your wash will have a higher specific gravity and be more prone to picking up color when heated. It is best to keep the specific gravity under 1.064 when boiling, and even this might be pushing it a bit if you are trying for clear (not slightly yellowed) base.

A short boil, around 15 minutes, is all you need. If you are confident in your ability to maintain a steady temperature with your kettle, you can hold the wash at 170°F (77°C) for 15 minutes to pasteurize it. You are not extracting bitterness from hops—even if you add hops, you do not want any perceptible hop bitterness in a hard seltzer. You are not coagulating proteins, as would be required in a brewery boil. All you really need to do is sanitize the wort and perhaps bubble out any volatile compounds. You should add a small amount of yeast nutrients at this point. You can do so any time within the first 10 minutes of the boil. For 5.0 gal. (19 L) of sugar wash, you will need of total of about 2 tsp. diammonium phosphate (DAP) and 1 tsp. complete yeast nutrients. Your recipe may specify breaking this amount into aliquots and adding part of it later, but the first dose should be added in the boil.

After the boil, the sugar wash should be chilled quickly. A submersible wort chiller will work well for this. If you, like me, live somewhere where the groundwater is fairly warm, adding a pre-chiller will help. A pre-chiller is another wort chiller in line between the tap and the main wort chiller. The pre-chiller sits in a bucket or other vessel to which ice water is added. This cools down the water that flows to the main chiller. When using a pre-chiller, hold off adding the ice until the sugar wash has chilled significantly. If you can touch the outside kettle and it does not feel particularly warm or cold, it is right around human body temperature. (Be very careful and do not touch the kettle until the wash has been cooling for a while.) For 5.0 gal. (19 L) batch of hard seltzer, a 10 lb. (4.5 kg) bag of ice will help you quickly get from around 100°F (38°C) to the mid-60s Fahrenheit (~18°C).

A counterflow wort chiller or plate chiller can also be used. If a pre-chiller is used, the ice should be added to the pre-chiller water throughout the entire process. Adjust the flow of water through the chiller and the flow of wash out of the kettle so the liquid entering the fermentor is at the correct temperature. Some chillers of this type also allow you to aerate the chilled wort as it exits the chiller.

A workable, but far less elegant, solution is to chill the wash in a large sink or bathtub filled with cold water. If you cool the wash in a sink, you will have to change the water multiple times until the side of the pot feels as if it is roughly body temperature. (Do not touch the pot until the water has been changed at least three times and 15 minutes has elapsed. Even then, be careful.) Once the pot has been cooled to that point with tap water, add ice to the next couple batches of cooling water. Keep the lid on the pot at all times during cooling, regardless of what method you use. This blocks airborne microorganisms from falling into the wash.

AERATION, OXYGENATION, AND pH ADJUSTMENT

No matter what method of chilling you used, the wash needs to be chilled, transferred to the fermentor, and aerated. A small oxygen tank connected via tubing to a HEPA filter that is, in turn, connected to a sintered aeration stone can be used for this. Most homebrew stores sell kits with everything you need except the oxygen tank. Those can be found at hardware stores with the welding equipment.

pH ADJUSTMENT

There is an optional step at this point in the process after chilling: pH adjustment. When wort is boiled, the pH typically drops to 5.0–5.2. Likewise, the pH of wine must is often in the 3.3–3.5 range. A solution of sugar and water will have a pH that is higher than either of these. When the sugar wash is fermented its pH will drop. However, you can adjust the pH prior to the fermentation if you wish to give the yeast a less stressful initial environment.

Sugar, whether glucose or sucrose, is not acidic or basic and does not contribute to the pH of the solution it is in. Thus, a mixture of pure sugar and pure water will simply be the pH of the water. If you used pure water, the pH will be 7. The pH of tap water might be different depending on what is dissolved in it. Most municipal water sources deliver water between pH 6.5 and 8.5, with a value around pH 8.1 being common. A sugar and water solution does not act as a pH buffer either. As such, a relatively small amount of acid added to a sugar wash will change its pH substantially. So, although the yeast might initially be slightly stressed by a high pH, the lactic acid produced during fermentation will quickly drop the pH into a more comfortable range. Still, some commercial producers adjust the pH of their wash and homebrewers can too.

To adjust the pH, use food-grade phosphoric acid or lactic acid. Take the pH of your sugar wash and, if it is out of the range you are shooting for, add a drop of acid. Stir the solution, wait 30 seconds or so, and take the pH again. Add acid drop by drop until you hit your desired range.

OXYGENATION

To aerate with oxygen, sanitize the tubing leading to the aeration stone and the stone itself by soaking in sanitizing solution. Drop the stone into the chilled sugar wash and let it sink to the bottom. Slowly turn the regulator knob on the oxygen rig until bubbles emerge from the aeration stone. Adjust the flow so the bubbles are small and there is only a small ripple at the surface of the liquid. If large bubbles are popping at the top, that means oxygen is just passing through the solution. One minute of oxygenation is all that is needed to reach the desired dissolved oxygen level of 6–8 ppm. If you can manage it, gently swirling the fermentor as you add oxygen will help the gas dissolve slightly better. (It makes the path of a bubble from the stone to the top slightly longer, a helix rather a straight line.)

You can also aerate with your stone connected to an aquarium pump. Air contains about 21% oxygen. So, when aerating with air, you need to bubble more gas through your wash. Aerating for 7–8 minutes with air should do the trick. As with oxygen, a stream of small bubbles that only makes a ripple at the top—not a bunch of fizz—is what you want.

PITCHING THE YEAST

Once the sugar wash is prepared—boiled, cooled, aerated, and (optionally) pH adjusted—it is time to pitch the yeast. Dried yeast can be sprinkled on top of the liquid, allowed to sit for about 5 minutes, then stirred into solution. Alternatively, the yeast can be rehydrated first in hot water, then cooled, and pitched. Different yeast strains have different requirements for rehydration—including temperatures and amounts of water required—and these are usually printed right on the sachet. Done properly, rehydration yields a higher percentage of healthy yeast cells compared to sprinkling dried yeast onto a sugar solution. Done incorrectly, for example, by pouring still-hot yeast into a cool solution, it actually decreases the number of healthy cells.

If you made a yeast starter, give it a whiff and see if it smells as a yeast starter should. (How should a yeast starter smell? That depends on the yeast strain.) If there is a layer of yeast on the bottom and clear liquid above it, carefully pour off as much of the supernatant (the clear liquid) as is possible, swirl the yeast, and dump it in the sugar wash. Pouring off the supernatant gets rid of any color it may be carrying, especially if it was made with some wort or grape juice. Pour the yeast starter supernatant into a glass and give it a taste, to check for signs of contamination. If the yeast starter is cloudy, the yeast is still in suspension and you will have to pitch the whole starter.

Once the yeast has been pitched, affix the airlock and move the fermentor somewhere where the temperature can be controlled. The optimal fermentation temperature will depend on the strain of yeast being used. Ideally, you want to conduct a fermentation that is as "clean" as possible. If you are using a neutral brewer's yeast, ferment in the mid-to-low range of the strain's recommended temperature range. Wine yeasts and distiller's yeasts are less finicky, but the temperature should be maintained such that the fermentation is orderly and not allowed to rise higher than a comparable wine fermentation would.

FERMENTATION

If you have pitched an adequate amount of healthy yeast, evidence of active fermentation should start by the next day. It may start sooner with some types of yeasts. During active fermentation, all the brewer needs to do is monitor the situation and ensure that the temperature stays within its prescribed bounds. Fermentations generate heat and you may see a spike early on. As fermentation proceeds, you may detect some unusual odors coming from the airlock. Hydrogen sulfide (H2S) is the most common off-odor that is found in sluggish hard seltzer fermentations. But a small amount is normal, especially in lager fermentations. With some yeast strains, certain off-putting aromas may be normal. If you are brewing your first hard seltzer, do not panic and dump a batch based on the odors emanating from the airlock. Do make sure to note the odors, the yeast strain you are using, the temperature, and how many hours fermentation has progressed, in your brewing notebook. This will help you interpret airlock odors the next time you brew.

Fermentation should peak during the first or second day of fermentation. With most yeast strains, it will be the first. This is a good time to add a second dose of yeast nutrients, if your recipe calls for it. The idea behind staggering the yeast nutrient additions is that the yeast will have taken in the initial dose and be ready—or almost so—for fresh nutrients. To add the second dose, place the yeast nutrient mixture in a small pan and add just enough water to make a fairly thick slurry. Gradually heat the mix. You can either simmer the mixture for about a minute or hold the mixture above 170°F (77°C) for a couple minutes and it will be sanitized. Let the mixture cool, swirl it around in the pan, and dump it into the fermentor. Your recipe will likely specify when to add yeast nutrients and in what amounts.

In the day or two after visible fermentation peaks, you will have to decide whether to add a third dose of yeast nutrients. If the yeast cells have depleted both of the previous additions, or nearly so, they may benefit from a third dose. On the other hand, if they have received all the nutrients they need to complete the fermentation, adding more nutrients will not help the yeast but they will be available to contaminating microorganisms. As a homebrewer, this decision will always involve some guesswork.

As fermentation progresses, the amount of CO_2 given off decreases as the fermentable sugars are consumed. If the fermentation is struggling, for example, because the yeast is lacking in nutrients, the amount of CO_2 production may drop drastically. Being able to distinguish between an ordinary slowing of fermentation, which can be occur quickly, and a sharp drop-off is difficult.

With hard seltzers, your best approach may be to smell the gases exiting the airlock. If they smell strongly of hydrogen sulfide, which smells like rotten eggs, that is a sign the yeast is struggling. However, some yeast strains produce a lot of hydrogen sulfide in a healthy fermentation. If your yeast starter smelled of hydrogen sulfide but the starter liquid tasted fine, then hydrogen sulfide at this stage may be normal. Unless you are reasonably sure that the fermentation is struggling or stalled, withholding yeast nutrients at this stage is probably the best approach.

In most cases, your hard seltzer fermentation should complete in 6–8 days. The amount of time required depends primarily on the amount of yeast pitched, the temperature of the fermentation, the yeast strain, the extent of aeration, and yeast nutrition. With starting gravities less than 1.040 SG, the yeast should work quickly if it is healthy and abundant. Allow the fermentation to slow to a stop and let the fermented wash sit, undisturbed, for at least a few days afterwards. This will give the yeast time to flocculate and take up some yeast by-products, such as diacetyl.

If your fermentation does become sluggish, you may want to rouse the yeast, raise the temperature of the fermentation slightly, or both. You can rouse the yeast by stirring the solution or swirling the fermentor. If the fermentation turned sluggish early, that is, before the first one-third of the sugar is consumed, adding additional yeast nutrients may help. Oxygenating after fermentation is likely to produce an excess of diacetyl and should be avoided.

Your fermentation should have produced a solution that is mostly water and 4%–5% alcohol. However, there are likely other compounds in the mix that may have an odor, flavor, and color. Removing these unwanted compounds will make for a better hard seltzer. A quick taste test will reveal how much intervention is required.

TASTE TEST

If you taste your fermented sugar wash and it smells and tastes "neutral," like water with a little alcohol and no strong off-odors or flavors, you can skip the following procedures and add your flavoring and acids. This is doubly true if the fermented wash is additionally low in color. As a homebrewer, your hard seltzer does not have to be crystal clear and absolutely flavorless. You can be the judge of whether your result is "close enough" and you wish to avoid the hassle of cleaning it up. Remember also that small amounts of off-odors and flavors, depending on what they are, may be at least partially hidden by the flavoring. Certainly, if your fermented wash smells slightly estery, and your flavoring is fruit based, the esters likely will not be a major problem. Flavors or aromas that are strong, offensive, or both will not be obscured by flavor additions. Small amounts of color in the wash may not be detrimental, especially with some flavorings that may also add some color. Large amounts of color, which in this case would be anything light Pilsner colored or darker, are problematic.

FINING

There are a variety of fining agents that homebrewers and home winemakers are familiar with. Two that can be very helpful when brewing a hard seltzer are activated carbon and polyvinylpolypyrrolidone (PVPP). Activated carbon is sometimes used to fine wines for off-flavors, off-odors, and color, but it is fairly non-specific. PVPP is usually used to fine alcoholic beverages for excess tannins, which should not be a problem in hard seltzers, but also removes bitter compounds. Used together, activated carbon and PVPP have the reputation of "stripping" wine of flavor and color. For a hard seltzer, for which you want a neutral base as beverage, this is a good thing.

Activated carbon is often mixed in a thick (10% w/v) slurry and used at a dosage of 50–2,000 mg/L. For 5.0 gal. (19 L) of hard seltzer, that would be 0.034–7.1 oz. (0.95–200 g). At the lower end of this range, activated carbon removes odors; at the higher end, it removes colors. Activated carbon falls out of solution and settles in less than an hour. Take care when mixing the slurry and dosing the beer. Activated carbon can be messy.

PVPP is dissolved in hot water and added at concentrations of 100–800 mg/L. For 5.0 gal. (19 L) of hard seltzer, this would be 0.067 to 0.53 ounces (1.9–15 g). Most types of PVPP will settle out in about six hours. Working together, you can fine with both activated carbon and PVPP in one day and then rack the clarified wash to a secondary fermentor that evening or the next day, leaving the fining agents behind as best you can in the primary fermentor. You may lose a tiny amount of liquid doing this.

For a homebrewed hard seltzer, one approach to fining would be to first assess the base beverage. It is pretty close to neutral and colorless? Does it have a few off-odors and a little unwanted color? Or is it problematic, showing strong off-odors or flavors and far too much color? For a "pretty close" beverage, fine with activated carbon at 0.034 oz. (0.95 g) per 5.0 gal. (19 L) followed by 0.067 oz. (1.9 g) of PVPP. For a problematic batch, fine with 7.1 oz. (200 g) of activated carbon per 5.0 gal. (19 L) and 0.53 oz. (15 g) of PVPP. For intermediate batches, use a rate between these based on whether you think it is closer to either of the two ends of the spectrum. You cannot mistakenly over-fine, so if you err on the side of using more finings, the only downside is the cost of the finings used. Also, if you fine the base beverage once and it improves but still shows problems, you can fine again.

There are other finings used in winemaking and beer making, but carbon and PVPP are easy to mix and use, are fast-acting, and have the reputation of being effective in removing odors and color when used together.

Filtering the neutral base will yield a clearer beverage. However, most homebrewers do not have the equipment for filtration. If you do, the best approach is to perform a coarse filtration to remove the yeast and other large particles, if present. Next, a finer filtration, preferably through filter pads that contain activated carbon, will produce a more polished beverage.

ODOR REMOVAL WITH CO$_2$

If your base beverage is good except for a small amount of unwanted odor, you have an option besides fining, which is bubbling CO$_2$ through the solution to scrub the volatile compounds responsible for the odor. To do this, you will need an aeration stone attached to your CO$_2$ tank. You will also need to knock as much CO$_2$ out of solution before you start as is feasible. Immediately after fermentation, your base beverage will be saturated with CO$_2$. If you bubble CO$_2$ through a solution already saturated with CO$_2$, it will foam extensively.

To remove CO$_2$ from your base beverage, take a sanitized long-handled spoon and stir the liquid, initially in a circular motion. It should start to form a whirlpool in the fermentation vessel. Then—while still stirring in the circle— move the spoon up and down to bring the bottom layers of the solution to the top as the solution rotates. Do not stir so vigorously that you whip air into the mix. Avoid splashing as far as you reasonably can. You want to let CO$_2$ out but not let oxygen in. Stir for a few minutes or, if you see bubbles rising to the surface, until the rate of bubbling diminishes.

Sanitize the stone and the tubing that leads to it and let the stone sink to the bottom of the vessel. Turn the gas on as slowly as you can reasonably manage and be ready to turn it off immediately if excessive foaming occurs. Adjust the flow of CO$_2$ bubbles coming from the aeration stone so it is just a trickle at first. Swirl the fermentor, if possible, being watchful that it does not start to foam uncontrollably. Once you can see the flow of bubbles is not causing a lot of foaming, turn the CO$_2$ up very slowly and bubble CO$_2$ through the solution for a couple minutes. Grasp the tubing leading to the stone and move it around so bubbles rise through all the different regions in the fermentor. Swirling the fermentor gently as the bubbles rise will help.

After bubbling the base beverage, you can taste test it again and see if this cleared up the problem. If not, you may want to try carbon fining and perhaps another round of bubbling. Obviously, avoiding problems in your fermentation is going to be a lot easier than cleaning them up afterward.

FLAVOR ADDITIONS AND CARBONATION

Once the wash is fermented and cleaned up, if needed, the next steps are flavor additions, back sweetening, stabilization, and carbonation. In a home brewery, it may be more convenient to leave carbonation as the last step. The big decision you need to make is whether you will force carbonate the batch or bottle condition it.

Hard seltzers are generally flavored with one or two different flavors and these should be stirred into solution at this point. The amount of each flavoring will be specified by the recipe, but it will not occupy a large volume. So, unless you are extremely exacting and want your hard seltzer to occupy 5.000 gallons (18.93 L) exactly, you do not need to worry about the tiny bit this will dilute your beverage. Once the flavoring is stirred in, add any acid that is called for. Do not mix these two together and then add them—add one and then the other. The order does not matter. The flavoring solution should be sanitary if the package has not been opened. Even if the flavoring has been used, if it is promptly closed and refrigerated it should be fine to use again. As for acid powders, like citric acid or malic acid, contaminating microorganisms cannot live on them in the absence of water. Additionally, the alcohol content and low pH of the presumptive hard seltzer will guard it against tiny amounts of contamination.

The next addition is the sugar for back sweetening. Back sweetening is only an option if you stabilize and force carbonate the beverage. You cannot back sweeten and bottle condition.

You may want to dilute the sugar in water and simmer it briefly to sanitize it. On the other hand, the alcohol and the low pH of the fermented solution make it unlikely that a sugar addition will contaminate the beverage. Once sugar is added any yeast remaining in solution can begin fermenting it, which is why the potassium sorbate stabilizer is necessary. For 5.0 gal. (19 L) of homebrewed hard seltzer, only 2.5 tsp. of potassium sorbate is needed. The addition of potassium sorbate keeps the yeast from "reawakening" (it will not stop an active fermentation, however, at this dosage).

Keep in mind that, if tasting a sample at this stage, the beverage is not carbonated and this will affect the final flavor. Carbonation will "brighten up" the flavor and make it seem crisper. If you have back sweetened and added potassium sorbate to stabilize the solution, you must force carbonate the hard seltzer. Any of the methods that work with homebrewed beer will work, including letting the keg sit under the appropriate CO_2 pressure for a while, or cranking up the pressure and shaking the keg. For 2.8 volumes of CO_2 at 40°F (4.4°C, i.e., usual refrigerator temperature), your gauge pressure should be 15–16 psi. You may also choose to carbonate and serve your hard seltzer at normal craft beer carbonation levels, typically 2.5 volumes CO_2. This will ensure you do not encounter any issue with foaming or other symptoms of an unbalanced draught system. (Many brewpubs do this.) To carbonate to 2.5 volumes of CO_2 you will need a gauge pressure of 12–13 psi for a beverage at 40°F (4.4°C). Note that any tubing in your draught system may retain a hint of whatever flavoring was used in the hard seltzer.

If you do not back sweeten you can bottle condition your hard seltzer. The mechanics are exactly the same as bottle conditioning homebrew: add sugar to the beverage and let the yeast ferment that sugar in the bottle. The carbon dioxide produced during fermentation will be trapped and carbonate the beverage. After fermentation, the sugar wash is saturated with carbon dioxide. At the atmospheric pressure in your residence, the liquid holds as much carbon dioxide as it can. Temperature also plays a role, because the cooler the temperature of your hard seltzer base beverage the more carbon dioxide it will hold. So, the amount of priming sugar to add depends both on your target level of carbonation and the degree to which it is already carbonated. Use tables 7.1 and 7.2 to estimate how much sugar you will need. For example, if you fermented your hard seltzer base at 65°F (18°C), it will have 0.89 volumes of CO_2 in it. To reach 2.8 volumes, you will need to add 1.9 volumes of CO_2. This corresponds to 5.5 oz. (160 g) of glucose in a 5.0 gal. (19 L) batch. Beware of adding too much priming sugar and overcarbonating the beverage—glass bottles can explode.

Table 7.1 Residual dissolved CO_2 at various temperatures

Temp (°F)	Temp (°C)	CO_2 (volumes)
50	10.0	1.15
51	10.6	1.13
52	11.1	1.11
53	11.7	1.09
54	12.2	1.08
55	12.8	1.06
56	13.3	1.04
57	13.9	1.02
58	14.4	1.01
59	15.0	0.99
60	15.6	0.97
61	16.1	0.96
62	16.7	0.94
63	17.2	0.92
64	17.8	0.91
65	18.3	0.89
66	18.9	0.88
67	19.4	0.86
68	20.0	0.85
69	20.6	0.83
70	21.1	0.82
71	21.7	0.81
72	22.2	0.79
73	22.8	0.78
74	23.3	0.77
75	23.9	0.75
76	24.4	0.74
77	25.0	0.73
78	25.6	0.72
79	26.1	0.70
80	26.7	0.69
81	27.2	0.68
82	27.8	0.67
83	28.3	0.66
84	28.9	0.65
85	29.4	0.64

Table 7.2 Volumes carbon dioxide produced in
5 gal. (19 L) of beer by priming sugar added

Sugar (oz.)	Sugar (g)	CO$_2$ produced (volumes)
0.25	7	0.09
0.50	14	0.17
0.75	21	0.26
1.00	28	0.34
1.25	35	0.43
1.50	43	0.51
1.75	50	0.60
2.00	57	0.68
2.25	64	0.77
2.50	71	0.85
2.75	78	0.94
3.00	85	1.02
3.25	92	1.10
3.50	99	1.19
3.75	106	1.27
4.00	113	1.36
4.25	121	1.44
4.50	128	1.53
4.75	135	1.61
5.00	142	1.70
5.25	149	1.78
5.50	156	1.87
5.75	163	1.95
6.00	170	2.04
6.25	177	2.12
6.50	184	2.20
6.75	191	2.29
7.00	199	2.37
7.25	206	2.46
7.50	213	2.54
7.75	220	2.63
8.00	227	2.71
priming sugar = glucose monohydrate (corn sugar)		

RECIPES AND OPTIONS

The recipe chapter (chap. 8) gives recipes for various hard seltzers at the home-brew scale. You will notice that most are very similar. As a homebrewer, you have the option to try different twists on the hard seltzer theme. Here are a few.

A SWEET MALTERNATIVE BEVERAGE

This is the most obvious twist on a hard seltzer. A sweeter, more flavorful drink, similar to "old-school" malternative beverages. To brew a beverage like this, all you really need to do is add more sugar to back sweeten and increase the amount of flavoring and acid. You will need to add potassium sorbate to stabilize a sweet malternative beverage, so this option is only available to homebrewers who can force carbonate and keg their beers.

A VERY DRY BEER

Hard seltzers are typically dry beverages. There are several beer styles also known for being dry. Brut IPA, which is a very dry pale ale, is one recent beer type that has gained some popularity. Dry stouts and some Belgian specialty ales, including tripel, are also known for being (at least relatively) dry. It is possible to concoct a recipe in which about half of the fermentables come from malted grains and half come from sugar. Exogenous enzymes reduce the carbohydrates in the wort or beer to simple sugars, as is done in brut IPA, and the result will be a super-dry, very pale beer. Adding fruit flavor is an option but the beverage can be unflavored.

Making a hard seltzer is well within the ability of any accomplished homebrewer on any "regular" homebrewing set-up. Hard seltzer brewing begins with making a flavorless and (nearly) colorless base beverage by fermenting a sugar wash, which is a mixture of sugar and water. The water used should be treated—as homebrewing water always should be—and also carefully taste tested. The initial density of the sugar wash should be 1.031–1.038 SG. In this range, the final alcohol content of the beverage will be 4%–5% ABV. The sugar wash is boiled and cooled, then the yeast is pitched. In order to help the yeast perform, yeast nutrients are added. After fermentation, the (hopefully) neutral base beverage is smelled and tasted. If off-odors or off-flavors are present, the solution can be fined. In the case of off-odors, CO_2 can be bubbled through the solution. Even color can be removed by fining with (relatively) large amounts of activated carbon. Once the base beverage is cleaned up, if needed, the flavor and acid (if any) are added and it is carbonated—typically to a fizzy 2.8 volumes of CO_2.

The most difficult aspect of brewing a hard seltzer is setting the conditions to allow the yeast to conduct an ordered fermentation. The better your fermentation is run, the less intervention will be required to clean the base beverage. The rest is just mixing flavors, sugars, and acids to the appropriate level.

© Brewers Association/Luke Trautwein

RECIPES FOR HOMEBREWERS

IN CHAPTER 7, I DISCUSSED how you can brew hard seltzers at home. Here I give homebrew recipes for many of the popular hard seltzer types. The flavors in these are interchangeable. The volume of flavoring you need to add will vary depending on the flavor. However, the difference in amounts is small enough that any dilution effects can be ignored. Of course, you can tweak the level of flavoring, acidity, and back sweetening to suit your tastes. The recipes are formulated to fit the mold of commercial hard seltzer examples. I also give recipes for two strong neutral bases that can be diluted to working strength.

The biggest key to success with these recipes is giving the yeast enough nutrients to vigorously ferment the sugar solution. The pitching rate and temperature recommendations should also be followed so that the fermentation is orderly and finishes with nearly all of the sugars being consumed.

The final specific gravity of these beverages should be below 1.000, around 0.997 in most cases. (The specific gravity can drop below 1.000 because ethanol is less dense than water, which, by definition, has a specific gravity of 1.000.)

Fining with activated carbon, or other fining agents, can help clear up unwanted odors, flavors, and even colors. However, if you run an ordered fermentation you may not need to do this step. Taste your neutral base before deciding to fine the solution.

These recipes can be scaled up or down, as needed. Just multiply the amount of every ingredient by your intended batch size (in either gallons or liters) then divide by 5.0 gal. (or 19 L), the volume of these recipes. For example, if you want to brew 2.5 gal. (9.5 L), multiply the amount of every ingredient by 2.5 (or 9.5) then divide by five (or 19). The units for volume will cancel, leaving the unit of measurement in the ingredients list.

You can substitute fruit or fruit juices for the flavorings, if you wish. In most beers, 1.0–2.0 lb. per gallon (120–240 g/L) is the range for fruit additions. For hard seltzers, about one-quarter to one-third of this rate is appropriate unless you are trying to make a more flavorful version. To add real fruit, brew the beverage at working strength. The best way to add fruit for this purpose is either as a puree or as juice. Be sure to account for the volume of the fruit addition when making the sugar solution. Dissolve the sugar to make a volume that your fruit addition will bring up to 5.0 gal. (19 L). Boil and cool, adding yeast nutrients where appropriate, then add the fruit to bring the mixture up to your batch size. Pitch your yeast and ferment. You can also wait to add the fruit until the sugar mixture has almost finished fermenting; the fermentation will briefly be renewed in this case. Either way, package as usual (for hard seltzers) when the fermentation is finished. The trace nutrients in fruit should help the yeast somewhat, but do not omit the yeast nutrients. (Do, obviously, omit the flavoring.) A final option is to add the fruit juice after fermentation is completely finished and add potassium sorbate to prevent a renewed fermentation. This may make the beverage sweeter than commercial examples.

You do not need to boil a full volume of sugar solution. You can add all the sugar required for a 5.0 gal. (19 L) batch into 2.5–3.0 gal. (9.5–11 L) of water. After boiling and cooling, transfer the sugar solution to your fermentor and top up to five gallons with cool water. This is essentially what is done when brewing stovetop extract beers. Boiling smaller volumes of sugar solution at higher concentrations of sugar may turn the liquid yellow.

RECIPES

HARD SELTZER RECIPES

STANDARD 4% ABV HARD SELTZER
For 5 US gallons (19 L)

Calories per serving: 90 (est.)
Flavor: lime

SELTZER INGREDIENTS
5.0 gal. (19 L) 4.0% ABV neutral base
0.95 fl. oz. (28 mL) lime flavoring
citric acid (to taste)
3.7 oz. (110 g) sucrose (for back sweetening)
0.13 oz. (3.7 g) potassium sorbate
6.0 oz. (170 g) corn sugar (for bottle carbonation)

4% NEUTRAL BASE INGREDIENTS
3.5 lb. (1.6 kg) sucrose
phosphoric acid (for pH adjustment)
113 billion cells yeast (1 qt. or 1 L yeast starter)
0.21 oz. (6.0 g) yeast nutrients

PROCEDURES FOR SELTZER
In a large, sanitized bucket, dilute an appropriate amount of your strong neutral base to the desired batch size at 4% ABV. Or brew the 4% neutral base with the amount of sugar listed (per 5.0 gal., or per 19 L) and transfer to a bucket. Add the flavoring, acid (if needed), and sucrose for back sweetening. After those are dissolved, add the potassium sorbate to prevent fermentation of the sweetening sugar. Rack to a keg and carbonate to 2.8 volumes of CO_2. You may also carbonate the beverage to normal beer levels so you do not need to balance your draught system. If bottling, do not add the sugar for back sweetening or the potassium sorbate. Use heavy bottles, such as those in which hefeweizens are packaged.

PROCEDURES FOR 4% ABV NEUTRAL BASE
To ferment your neutral base at working strength, follow these instructions. Fill your kettle with 4.0 gal. (15 L) of water. Add the correct amount of sugar

and stir until dissolved. Add water to top up to 5.0 gal. (19 L). Check the density with a hydrometer or refractometer, it should read 1.032 SG or 8°Bx. Check the pH and adjust to an appropriate pH for your yeast, if desired. (This is around pH 5 for beer yeasts or pH 4 for wine yeasts.)

Bring the sugar solution to a boil and boil gently for 5 minutes (this should not boil off a significant volume of water). Cool the sugar solution, aerate the mixture, and transfer to your fermentor. Pitch the yeast and add the yeast nutrients. Ferment in the middle of the temperature range specified for your yeast strain. For most neutral ale strains, 65–68°F (18–20°C) will work. Wine strains can ferment at much higher temperatures, up to 80°F (27°C). As the fermentation nears its conclusion, you may want to swirl the fermentor gently for a few times each day or allow the temperature to rise slightly. Do not exceed the yeast strain's recommended working temperature range.

After fermentation, you may want to either fine with activated carbon or some other fining agent. With proper yeast nutrition, fermenting a low-gravity solution such as this should not put much stress on the yeast so you may not have any off-aromas or flavors to address. Once your base is brewed and cleaned up, proceed to adding the remaining ingredients as described above for the seltzer ingredients and procedures.

STANDARD 5% ABV HARD SELTZER

For 5 US gallons (19 L)

Calories per serving: 100 (est.)
Flavor: cherry

SELTZER INGREDIENTS

5.0 gal. (19 L) 5.0% ABV neutral base
0.82 fl. oz. (24 mL) cherry flavoring
malic acid (to taste)
1.9 oz. (54 g) sucrose (for back sweetening)
0.13 oz. (3.7 g) potassium sorbate
6.0 oz. (170 g) corn sugar (for bottle carbonation)

5% NEUTRAL BASE INGREDIENTS

4.30 lb. (1.95 kg) sucrose
phosphoric acid (for pH adjustment)
142 billion cells yeast (1 qt. or 1 L yeast starter)
0.23 oz. (6.5 g) yeast nutrients

PROCEDURES FOR SELTZER

In a large, sanitized bucket, dilute an appropriate amount of your strong neutral base to the desired batch size at 5% ABV. Or brew the 5% neutral base with the amount of sugar listed (per 5.0 gal. or per 19 L) and transfer to a bucket. Add the flavoring, acid (if needed), and sucrose for back sweetening. After those are dissolved, add the potassium sorbate to prevent fermentation of the sweetening sugar. Rack to a keg and carbonate to 2.8 volumes of CO_2. You may also carbonate the beverage to normal beer levels so you do not need to balance your draught system. If bottling, do not add the sugar for back sweetening or the potassium sorbate. Use heavy bottles, such as those in which hefeweizens are packaged.

PROCEDURES FOR 5% ABV NEUTRAL BASE

To ferment your neutral base at working strength, follow these instructions. Fill your kettle with 4.0 gal. (15 L) of water. Add the correct amount of sugar and stir until dissolved. Add water to top up to 5.0 gal. (19 L). Check the density with a hydrometer or refractometer, it should read 1.040 SG or 10°Bx. Check the pH and adjust to an appropriate pH for your yeast, if desired. (This is around pH 5 for beer yeasts or pH 4 for wine yeasts.)

Bring the sugar solution to a boil and boil gently for 5 minutes (this should not boil off a significant volume of water). Cool the sugar solution, aerate the mixture, and transfer to your fermentor. Pitch the yeast and add the yeast nutrients. Ferment in the middle of the temperature range specified for your yeast strain. For most neutral ale strains, 65–68°F (18–20°C) will work. Wine strains can ferment at much higher temperatures, up to 80°F (27°C). As the fermentation nears its conclusion, you may want to swirl the fermentor gently for a few times each day or allow the temperature to rise slightly. Do not exceed the yeast strain's recommended working temperature range.

After fermentation, you may want to either fine with activated carbon or some other fining agent. With proper yeast nutrition, fermenting a low-gravity solution such as this should not put much stress on the yeast so you may not have any off-aromas or flavors to address. Once your base is brewed and cleaned up, proceed to adding the remaining ingredients as described above for seltzer ingredients and procedures.

SLIGHTLY SWEET 4% ABV
HARD SELTZER *For 5 US gallons (19 L)*

Calories per serving: 99 (est.)
Flavor: peach

SELTZER INGREDIENTS

5.0 gal. (19 L) 4.0% ABV neutral base
2.0 fl. oz. (60 mL) peach flavoring
malic acid (to taste)
8.1 oz. (230 g) sucrose (for back sweetening)
0.13 oz. (3.7 g) potassium sorbate
6.0 oz. (170 g) corn sugar (for bottle carbonation)

4% NEUTRAL BASE INGREDIENTS

3.5 lb. (1.6 kg) of sucrose
phosphoric acid (for pH adjustment)
113 billion cells yeast (1 qt. or 1 L yeast starter)
0.21 oz. (6.0 g) yeast nutrients

PROCEDURES FOR SELTZER

In a large, sanitized bucket, dilute an appropriate amount of your strong neutral base to the desired batch volume at 4% ABV. Or brew the 4% neutral base with the amount of sugar listed (per 5.0 gal. or per 19 L) and transfer to a bucket. Add the flavoring, acid (if needed), and sucrose for back sweetening. After those are dissolved, add the potassium sorbate to prevent fermentation of the sweetening sugar. Rack to a keg and carbonate to 2.8 volumes of CO_2. You may also carbonate the beverage to normal beer levels so you do not need to balance your draught system. If bottling, do not add the sugar for back sweetening or the potassium sorbate. Use heavy bottles, such as those in which hefeweizens are packaged. Without back sweetening, however, the beverage will not be sweet.

PROCEDURES FOR 4% ABV NEUTRAL BASE

To ferment your neutral base at working strength, follow these instructions. Fill your kettle with 4.0 gal. (15 L) of water. Add the correct amount of sugar and stir until dissolved. Add water to top up to 5.0 gal. (19 L). Check the density with a hydrometer or refractometer, it should read 1.032 SG or 8°Bx. Check the pH and adjust to an appropriate pH for your yeast, if desired. (This is around pH 5 for beer yeasts or pH 4 for wine yeasts.)

Bring the sugar solution to a boil and boil gently for 5 minutes (this should not boil off a significant volume of water). Cool the sugar solution, aerate the mixture, and transfer to your fermentor. Pitch the yeast and add the yeast nutrients. Ferment in the middle of the temperature range specified for your yeast strain. For most neutral ale strains, 65–68°F (18–20°C) will work. Wine strains can ferment at much higher temperatures, up to 80°F (27°C). As the fermentation nears its conclusion, you may want to swirl the fermentor gently for a few times each day or allow the temperature to rise slightly. Do not exceed the yeast strain's recommended working temperature range.

After fermentation, you may want to either fine with activated carbon or some other fining agent. With proper yeast nutrition, fermenting a low-gravity solution such as this should not put much stress on the yeast so you may not have any off-aromas or flavors to address. Once your base is brewed and cleaned up, proceed to adding the remaining ingredients as described above for seltzer ingredients and procedures.

SLIGHTLY SWEET 5% ABV
HARD SELTZER *For 5 US gallons (19 L)*

Calories per serving: 110 (est.)
Flavor: grapefruit

SELTZER INGREDIENTS
5.0 gal. (19 L) 5.0% ABV neutral base
0.82 fl. oz. (24 mL) flavoring
citric acid (to taste)
6.6 oz. (190 g) sucrose (for back sweetening)
0.13 oz. (3.7 g) potassium sorbate
6.0 oz. (170 g) corn sugar (for bottle carbonation)

5% NEUTRAL BASE INGREDIENTS
4.4 lb. (2.0 kg) sucrose
phosphoric acid (for pH adjustment)
142 billion cells yeast (1 qt. or 1 L yeast starter)
0.23 oz. (6.5 g) yeast nutrients

PROCEDURES FOR SELTZER
In a large, sanitized bucket, dilute an appropriate amount of your strong neutral base to the desired batch size at 5% ABV. Or brew the 5% neutral base

with the amount of sugar listed (per 5.0 gal., or per 19 L) and transfer to a bucket. Add the flavoring, acid (if needed), and sucrose for back sweetening. After those are dissolved, add the potassium sorbate to prevent fermentation of the sweetening sugar. Rack to a keg and carbonate to 2.8 volumes of CO_2. You may also carbonate the beverage to normal beer levels so you do not need to balance your draught system. If bottling, do not add the sugar for back sweetening or the potassium sorbate. Use heavy bottles, such as those in which hefeweizens are packaged. Without back sweetening, however, the beverage will not be sweet.

PROCEDURES FOR 5% ABV NEUTRAL BASE
To ferment your neutral base at working strength, follow these instructions. Fill your kettle with 4.0 gal. (15 L) of water. Add the correct amount of sugar and stir until dissolved. Add water to top up to 5.0 gal. (19 L). Check the density with a hydrometer or refractometer, it should read 1.040 SG or 10°Bx. Check the pH and adjust to an appropriate pH for your yeast, if desired. (This is around pH 5 for beer yeasts or pH 4 for wine yeasts.)

Bring the sugar solution to a boil and boil gently for 5 minutes (this should not boil off a significant volume of water). Cool the sugar solution, aerate the mixture, and transfer to your fermentor. Pitch the yeast and add the yeast nutrients. Ferment in the middle of the temperature range specified for your yeast strain. For most neutral ale strains, 65–68°F (18–20°C) will work. Wine strains can ferment at much higher temperatures, up to 80°F (27°C). As the fermentation nears its conclusion, you may want to swirl the fermentor gently for a few times each day or allow the temperature to rise slightly. Do not exceed the yeast strain's recommended working temperature range.

After fermentation, you may want to either fine with activated carbon or some other fining agent. With proper yeast nutrition, fermenting a low-gravity solution such as this should not put much stress on the yeast so you may not have any off-aromas or flavors to address. Once your base is brewed and cleaned up, proceed to adding the remaining ingredients as described above for seltzer ingredients and procedures.

EXTRA LOW CALORIE 3.5% ABV
HARD SELTZER *For 5 US gallons (19 L)*

Calories per serving: 70 (est.)
Flavor: pineapple

SELTZER INGREDIENTS
5.0 gal. (19 L) 3.5% ABV neutral base
1.5 fl. oz (44 mL) pineapple flavoring
malic acid (to taste)
1.9 oz. (54 g) sucrose (for back sweetening)
0.13 oz. (3.7 g) potassium sorbate
6.0 oz. (170 g) corn sugar (for bottle carbonation)

3.5% NEUTRAL BASE INGREDIENTS
3.1 lb. (1.4 kg) of sucrose
phosphoric acid (for pH adjustment)
100 billion cells yeast (1 qt. or 1 L yeast starter)
0.19 oz. (5.4 g) yeast nutrients

PROCEDURES FOR SELTZER
In a large, sanitized bucket, dilute an appropriate amount of your strong neutral base to the desired batch volume at 3.5% ABV. Or brew the 3.5% neutral base with the amount of sugar listed (per 5.0 gal., or per 19 L) and transfer to a bucket. Add the flavoring, acid (if needed), and sucrose for back sweetening. After those are dissolved, add the potassium sorbate to prevent fermentation of the sweetening sugar. Rack to a keg and carbonate to 2.8 volumes of CO_2. You may also carbonate the beverage to normal beer levels so you do not need to balance your draught system. If bottling, do not add the sugar for back sweetening or the potassium sorbate. Use heavy bottles, such as those in which hefeweizens are packaged.

PROCEDURES FOR 3.5% ABV NEUTRAL BASE
To ferment your neutral base at working strength, follow these instructions. Fill your kettle with 4.0 gal. (15 L) of water. Add the correct amount of sugar and stir until dissolved. Add water to top up to 5.0 gal. (19 L). Check the density with a hydrometer or refractometer, it should read 1.028 SG or 7°Bx. Check the pH and adjust to an appropriate pH for your yeast, if desired. (This is around pH 5 for beer yeasts or pH 4 for wine yeasts.)

Bring the sugar solution to a boil and boil gently for 5 minutes (this should not boil off a significant volume of water). Cool the sugar solution, aerate the mixture, and transfer to your fermentor. Pitch the yeast and add the yeast nutrients. Ferment in the middle of the temperature range specified for your yeast strain. For most neutral ale strains, 65–68°F (18–20°C) will work. Wine strains can ferment at much higher temperatures, up to 80°F (27°C). As the fermentation nears its conclusion, you may want to swirl the fermentor gently for a few times each day or allow the temperature to rise slightly. Do not exceed the yeast strain's recommended working temperature range.

After fermentation, you may want to either fine with activated carbon or some other fining agent. With proper yeast nutrition, fermenting a low-gravity solution such as this should not put much stress on the yeast so you may not have any off-aromas or flavors to address. Once your base is brewed and cleaned up, proceed to adding the remaining ingredients as described above for seltzer ingredients and procedures.

SLIGHTLY STRONGER 6% ABV
HARD SELTZER *For 5 US gallons (19 L)*

Calories per serving: 115 (est.)
Flavor: orange

SELTZER INGREDIENTS
5.0 gal. (19 L) 6.0% ABV neutral base
1.5 fl. oz. (44 mL) orange flavoring
citric acid (to taste)
1.9 oz. (54 g) sucrose (for back sweetening)
0.13 oz. (3.7 g) potassium sorbate
6.0 oz. (170 g) corn sugar (for bottle carbonation)

6.0% NEUTRAL BASE INGREDIENTS
5.2 lb. (2.3 kg) sucrose
phosphoric acid (for pH adjustment)
165 billion cells yeast (1.5 qt./1.5 L yeast starter)
0.24 oz. (6.9 g) yeast nutrients

PROCEDURES FOR SELTZER
In a large, sanitized bucket, dilute an appropriate amount of your strong neutral base to the desired batch volume at 6% ABV. Or brew the 6% neutral base

with the amount of sugar listed (per 5.0 gal., or per 19 L) and transfer to a bucket. Add the flavoring, acid (if needed), and sucrose for back sweetening. After those are dissolved, add the potassium sorbate to prevent fermentation of the sweetening sugar. Rack to a keg and carbonate to 2.8 volumes of CO_2. You may also carbonate the beverage to normal beer levels so you do not need to balance your draught system. If bottling, do not add the sugar for back sweetening or the potassium sorbate. Use heavy bottles, such as those in which hefeweizens are packaged.

PROCEDURES FOR 6% ABV NEUTRAL BASE

To ferment your neutral base at working strength, follow these instructions. Fill your kettle with 4.0 gal. (15 L) of water. Add the correct amount of sugar and stir until dissolved. Add water to top up to 5.0 gal. (19 L). Check the density with a hydrometer or refractometer, it should read 1.047 SG or 12°Bx. Check the pH and adjust to an appropriate pH for your yeast, if desired. (This is around pH 5 for beer yeasts or pH 4 for wine yeasts.)

Bring the sugar solution to a boil and boil gently for 5 minutes (this should not boil off a significant volume of water). Cool the sugar solution, aerate the mixture, and transfer to your fermentor. Pitch the yeast and add the yeast nutrients. Ferment in the middle of the temperature range specified for your yeast strain. For most neutral ale strains, 65–68°F (18–20°C) will work. Wine strains can ferment at much higher temperatures, up to 80°F (27°C). As the fermentation nears its conclusion, you may want to swirl the fermentor gently for a few times each day or allow the temperature to rise slightly. Do not exceed the yeast strain's recommended working temperature range.

After fermentation, you may want to either fine with activated carbon or some other fining agent. With proper yeast nutrition, fermenting a low-gravity solution such as this should not put much stress on the yeast so you may not have any off-aromas or flavors to address. Once your base is brewed and cleaned up, proceed to adding the remaining ingredients as described above for seltzer ingredients and procedures.

NEUTRAL BASE RECIPES

8% ABV NEUTRAL BASE *For 5 US gallons (19 L)*

When diluted 1:1 with de-aerated water, this neutral base can be used to generate twice its volume in 4% ABV hard seltzer.

INGREDIENTS

6.8 lb. (3.1 kg) sucrose

phosphoric acid (for pH adjustment)

225 billion cells yeast (2.5 qt. or 2.5 L yeast starter)

0.27 oz. (7.7 g) yeast nutrients

PROCEDURES

Mix the sucrose into 4.0 gal. (15 L) of water and stir to dissolve. Top up to your full volume. The density should be 1.063 SG or 16°Bx. Bring the mixture to a boil and boil for 5 minutes. Cool the sugar solution, transfer to a fermentor, and aerate thoroughly.

Pitch the yeast and add the yeast nutrients. Monitor the fermentation temperature and keep it in line with your yeast strain's recommended temperature. Near the end of fermentation, it may help to rouse the yeast by gently swirling the fermentor. You may also want to allow the temperature to rise a bit to help the yeast to finish.

Assess the neutral base and determine if you need to scrub any flavors or aromas. Bubbling CO_2 through the solution will knock out aromas. Filtering through or fining with activated carbon will remove flavors, aromas, and color. Five gallons (19 L) of this 8% ABV strong base will make 10 gal. (38 L) of 4% ABV neutral base when diluted with 5.0 gal. (19 L) of de-aerated water. Water can be de-aerated by boiling it vigorously, then cooling quickly with as little agitation as possible.

10% ABV NEUTRAL BASE *For 5 US gallons (19 L)*

When diluted 1:1 with de-aerated water, this neutral base can be used to generate twice its volume in 5% ABV hard seltzer.

INGREDIENTS

8.5 lb. (3.9 kg) sucrose
phosphoric acid (for pH adjustment)
290 billion cells yeast (4.5 qt. or 4.5 L yeast starter)
0.30 oz. (8.5 g) complete yeast nutrients

PROCEDURES

Mix the sucrose into 4.0 gal. (15 L) of water and stir to dissolve. Top up to your full volume. The density should be 1.078 SG or 19°Bx. Bring the mixture to a boil and boil for 5 minutes. Cool the sugar solution, transfer to a fermentor, and aerate thoroughly.

Pitch the yeast and add the yeast nutrients. Monitor the fermentation temperature and keep it in line with your yeast strain's recommended temperature. Near the end of fermentation, it may help to rouse the yeast by gently swirling the fermentor. You may also want to allow the temperature to rise a bit to help the yeast to finish.

Assess the neutral base and determine if you need to scrub any flavor or aromas. Bubbling CO_2 through the solution will knock out aromas. Filtering through or fining with activated carbon will remove flavors, aromas, and color.

Five gallons (19 L) of this 10% ABV strong base will make 10 gal. (38 L) of 5% ABV neutral base when diluted with 5.0 gal. (19 L) of de-aerated water. Water can be de-aerated by boiling it vigorously, then cooling quickly with as little agitation as possible.

© Getty/porosolka

9

SELTZER COCKTAILS ANYONE CAN MAKE

HARD SELTZERS ARE MEANT TO be simple beverages. Hard seltzer aficionados choose them as low-calorie, moderate-alcohol beverages without pretense. Still, there may be occasions when you want to do more than drink hard seltzer from a can or serve the beverage by itself in a glass. If you are hosting a party, or you are the manager at a brewpub that makes hard seltzer, finding ways to gussy up a plain-Jane hard seltzer may generate some interest from your guests. Below are some cocktails that you can mix up by using various ingredients to play with flavor and aroma. You can additionally garnish a hard seltzer cocktail—or even just a hard seltzer in a glass—with a slice of lime, a cherry, a sprig of mint, or any garnish that makes sense.

There are a number of simple things you can do to spruce up a hard seltzer. One of the most obvious is to make it sweeter. A typical hard seltzer only has a few grams of carbohydrates per 12 fl. oz. serving and this is reflected in their taste. Adding a bit of sugar can make the hard seltzer taste better, or at least sweeter. Even a small bump in the amount of sweetness can make a big difference. For example, taste a commercial hard seltzer that has 110 calories and 5 g of sugar per serving and compare it to a typical hard seltzer of the same alcohol content in the 90–100-calorie and 2 g of sugar range.

SIMPLE SYRUP

The easiest way to add sweetness is to use simple syrup. You can add granulated sugar to a hard seltzer, but this provides nucleation points for the dissolved CO_2 to come out of solution, lowering the carbonation level of the drink. Simple syrup is used by bartenders when making sweet cocktails. It is a 1:1 mixture of sugar and water by volume. One US fluid ounce (30 mL) of simple syrup contains 14 g of sugar and has 50 calories. A jigger, 1.5 fl. oz. (44 mL), has 21 g of sugar and 74 calories. As such, a single, one-ounce (30 mL) shot of simple syrup in a 12 fl. oz. (355 mL) serving of hard seltzer yields almost the same number of calories as a typical soda, but with only about a third of the sweetness from sugar. (The alcohol in the hard seltzer, you recall, is the source of most of its calories.) There are also flavored syrups used by bartenders and all of the popular fruit flavors can be found in this form.

SIMPLE SLIMON *For 1 serving*

Calories: 140–150
ABV: 4%–5%

INGREDIENTS
one 12 fl. oz. (355 mL) hard seltzer (lime flavor)
1.0 fl. oz. (30 mL) simple syrup

PROCEDURE
Stir 1.0 fl. oz. (30 mL, i.e., a shot) of simple syrup into a lime-flavored hard seltzer. Garnish with a wedge of lime, if desired.

SWEET CHERRY FIZZ *For 1 serving*

Calories: 164–174
ABV: 4%–5%

INGREDIENTS

one 12 fl. oz. (355 mL) hard seltzer (black cherry flavor)
1.5 fl. oz. (44 mL) cherry-flavored syrup

PROCEDURE

Stir one jigger (1.5 fl. oz., or 44 mL) of cherry-flavored syrup into a black cherry–flavored hard seltzer. Garnish with a maraschino cherry and a wedge of orange, if desired.

SOFT DRINKS

Another way to add sweetness, as well as some added flavor, is to blend some soda into a hard seltzer. A typical soda (or soft drink) contains 150–160 calories and 39–43 g of sugar per 12 fl. oz. serving. A single shot (1.0 fl. oz., or 30 mL) of soda contains 3.3–3.6 g of sugar and adds 12.5–13.3 calories; a jigger (1.5 fl. oz., or 44 mL) contains 4.9–5.4 g of sugar and adds 19–20 calories. This is about a quarter as much sugar per unit volume compared to simple syrup. A shot of soda will move the sweetness of a typical hard seltzer up a notch to roughly the level of sweetness that is found in, for example, Press hard seltzer brands.

In addition to sweetness, soda will add a bit of flavor. You can match the soft drink to the flavor of the hard seltzer or choose a flavor that blends well with the existing flavor of the hard seltzer. For example, any lemon-lime soda, such as 7-Up or Sprite, will work well in either a lime-flavored or lemon-flavored hard seltzer. Other citrus options are grapefruit-flavored sodas (most notably Squirt) and orange flavored sodas (including Sunkist, Crush Orange Soda, Orange Fanta, and—despite its green color—Mt. Dew). Cherry sodas include IBC Black Cherry, Crush Cherry Soda, and numerous "artisanal" soft drink brands. There are also soft drinks with cherry as one of the flavors, including Cherry Coke, Pepsi Wild Cherry, and Dr. Pepper.

While some soft drinks will add color to your cocktail, most are not cloudy and so the resulting mix will be clear. Overall, mixing a small amount of a soft drink into a hard seltzer is an easy way to boost the sweetness and flavor a bit, but still not end up with a soda-like sweetness. In addition, a shot or jigger of soda in a 12 fl. oz. hard seltzer is not going to greatly increase the caloric content. Blending a soft drink into hard seltzer will also give a cocktail with more carbonation than one made using non-carbonated liquids such as syrup or fruit juice.

OG GATOR *For 1 serving*

Calories: 103–113
ABV: 4%–5%

INGREDIENTS

one 12 fl. oz. (355 mL) hard seltzer (grapefruit flavor)
1.0 fl. oz. (30 mL) grapefruit-flavored soft drink

PROCEDURE

Stir one shot (1.0 fl. oz., or 30 mL) of grapefruit-flavored soft drink into a grapefruit-flavored hard seltzer. Garnish with an orange or grapefruit slice, if desired.

CREATURE FROM THE BLACK LAGOON *For 1 serving*

Calories: 109–119
ABV: 4%–5%

INGREDIENTS

one 12 fl. oz. (355 mL) hard seltzer (black cherry flavor)
1.5 fl. oz. (44 mL) black cherry–flavored soft drink

PROCEDURE

Stir one shot (1.0 fl. oz., or 30 mL) of black cherry–flavored soft drink into a black cherry–flavored hard seltzer. Garnish with a maraschino cherry, if desired.

C8 *For 1 serving*

Calories: 116–126
ABV: slightly less than 4%–5%

INGREDIENTS

one 12 fl. oz. (355 mL) hard seltzer (lime, lemon, or lemonade flavor)
2.0 fl. oz. (60 mL) lemon-lime–flavored soft drink

PROCEDURE

Stir two shots (2.0 fl. oz., or 60 mL) of lemon-lime–flavored soft drink into a
hard seltzer. Garnish with a wedge of lime, lemon, or both, if desired.

FRUIT JUICE

Another candidate for blending with hard seltzer is fruit juice. Fruit juices generally have a sugar content on par with soft drinks, although juices vary more
in this regard. Incorporating fruit juice into hard seltzer cocktails may appeal
to people who are attracted to natural, raw ingredients (but also hard seltzers
at the same time). With a fruit juicer, squeezing lemons, limes, or oranges is an
easier option. In most cases, the flavor of an actual fruit juice will round out
the flavor profile from the artificial fruit flavor in the hard seltzer. However,
sometimes the artificial flavor still dominates.

Orange juice can be paired with orange-flavored hard seltzer or, indeed,
any citrus fruit–flavored hard seltzer. The same applies to grapefruit juice.
Cherry juice obviously goes with cherry-flavored hard seltzer but also blends
well with lime. Cranberry juice is strongly flavored and works well in a cranberry hard seltzer, but will also work well with lime. Finally, apple juice and
grape juice are popular juices, but these flavors do not seem to be used in
commercial hard seltzers, probably due to makers wanting to avoid possible
confusion with ciders and wines. However, apple or grape juice will blend well
with either citrus flavors or selected other fruits.

Fruit juices will, of course, add color to your hard seltzer cocktail and may
diminish its clarity. This is unlikely to offend anyone. Added fruit juice will also
reduce the level of carbonation. In the case of small additions of fruit juice—a shot
or jigger in 12 fl. oz. (355 mL) of hard seltzer—this effect will be minimal. In mixes
with a higher juice to seltzer ratio, the beverage will be noticeably less fizzy.

When making hard seltzer and fruit juice cocktails, you can head in one
of two directions. As with soft drink mixes, you can add a little to nudge the
sweetness and flavor up a notch while still basically ending up with a hard

seltzer. Alternatively, you can use closer to a half-and-half mixture and make a "healthy," low-alcohol concoction. Hard seltzers are already low in alcohol and perceived as a healthy alternative to beer, wine, or mixed drinks. Viewed in this light, there may be people interested in taking it a step further with a more "natural" and lower-alcohol, though somewhat higher in calories, beverage.

CAPE SCROD *For 1 serving*

Calories: 109–119
ABV: 4%–5%

INGREDIENTS
one 12 fl. oz. (355 mL) hard seltzer (cranberry flavor)
1.5 fl. oz. (44 mL) cranberry juice

PROCEDURE
Stir one jigger (1.5 fl. oz., or 44 mL) of cranberry juice into a hard seltzer. Garnish with a wedge of lime or orange, if desired.

PLANET P *For 1 serving*

Calories: 103–113
ABV: 4%–5%

INGREDIENTS
one 12 fl. oz. (355 mL) hard seltzer (orange or clementine flavor)
1.0 fl. oz. (30 mL) pomegranate juice

PROCEDURE
Stir one shot (1.0 fl. oz., or 30 mL) of pomegranate juice into a hard seltzer. Garnish with a wedge of orange, if desired.

BEER

Most hard seltzers are brewed beverages. Beer is a brewed beverage. Why not combine the two, if you like? Arguably, the most famous beer cocktail is the shandy or *radler*, a beer mixed with a citrus beverage such as lemonade or limeade. The mix is usually half and half to produce a refreshing, low-alcohol cocktail. Mixing beer with a citrus-flavored hard seltzer will give a similar, though much less sweet, result.

Another famous beer cocktail is the *michelada*, a beer with tomato juice, lime juice, and chili peppers. Some versions contain Worcestershire sauce, soy sauce, or other flavorings. The salty, lightly sour drink is popular in Mexico, Latin America, and the US states along the Mexico–US border. By substituting a few ounces of lime hard seltzer for the small amount of lime juice in the recipe, and cutting back on the tomato juice a bit, you can make a "lean" michelada (i.e., one with fewer calories and less sweetness).

Berliner *weiss*—a very light, dry, sour wheat beer—is sometimes served with woodruff syrup or raspberry syrup. This gives the beer both some sweetness and flavor. A hard seltzer, of course, has almost no sweetness, but blending it with a sour beer can cut down on the tartness of the latter, if that is desired, and lend a little flavor. Additionally, adding sugar can result in an interesting hard seltzer and beer cocktail.

You can also just explore various mixes knowing that, in most cases, a 1:1 mix is going to produce a thinner, lower-calorie drink compared to the beer. Most average strength (~5% ABV) beers fall in the general ballpark of 150–190 calories per 12 fl. oz. (355 mL) serving. Light beers, of course, are less caloric, falling within a wide range of calorie counts—down to the 50s for some ultra-low-calorie beers.

VELODROME *For 2 servings*

Calories per serving: 125
ABV: roughly 5%

INGREDIENTS
one 12 fl. oz. (355 mL) Pilsner beer
one 12 fl. oz. (355 mL) hard seltzer (lemonade, lime, or lemon flavor)

PROCEDURE
Mix the beer and hard seltzer together.

MICHIGANA *For 3 servings*

Calories per serving: 130
ABV: roughly 5%

INGREDIENTS

two 12 fl. oz. (355 mL) Mexican lagers (Mexican-style lagers also work)
one 12 fl. oz. (355 mL) hard seltzer (lime flavored)
3 fl. oz. (90 mL) tomato juice
¼ fl. oz. (7 mL) Worcestershire sauce
½ fl. oz. (14 mL) hot sauce (e.g., Cholula Hot Sauce)

PROCEDURES

Mix the beer and hard seltzer together. Stir in the tomato juice, Worcestershire sauce, and hot sauce. Garnish with a lime and coat the rim of the glass with a 2:1 mixture of salt and chili powder, if desired.

WINE

Two well-known wine cocktails are the mimosa and sangria. Mimosa is champagne mixed with orange juice, whereas sangria is a blend of red wine and fruit. (Sangria is probably better described as a wine-based drink than a wine cocktail.) Either of these can be adapted to make a hard seltzer cocktail, and other possibilities exist as well.

Wine is higher in both calories and alcohol content. One fluid ounce (30 mL) of wine generally has around 25 calories, so a mixture of 6.0 fl. oz. (180 mL) wine and 6.0 fl. oz. hard seltzer will have roughly 200 calories and be 8%–9% ABV (this assumes the wine is 11%–14% ABV and the hard seltzer is 5% ABV.)

LOBIN REACH *For 2 servings*

Calories per serving: roughly 200
ABV: roughly 7.5% (exact value depends on the wine)

INGREDIENTS

one 12 fl. oz. (355 mL) hard seltzer (orange or clementine flavor)
12 fl. oz. (355 mL) sparkling wine

PROCEDURE

Mix the sparkling wine and hard seltzer together.

COZUMEL SUNSET *For 4 servings*

Calories per serving: roughly 212

ABV: roughly 7.5% (exact value depends on the wine)

INGREDIENTS

two 12 fl. oz. (355 mL) hard seltzers (one orange-flavored and one cherry-flavored)

one 750 mL bottle fruity red wine (9%–10% ABV)

1 tbsp sugar (optional)

sliced fruit (can include orange, lime, strawberries, cherries, apples, etc.)

PROCEDURES

Mix the hard seltzers and wine together. Stir in sugar, if you are using it. Add sliced fruit. Adding a jigger (1.5 fl. oz., or 44 mL) of brandy will make this closer to a traditional sangria.

HERBS AND FLOWERS

If you are making your own single-serving hard seltzers, you can also incorporate herbs or flowers into your mixture. If you bruise mint leaves, basil leaves, hibiscus flowers, or the like and add them, they will infuse the drink with their flavor and also add some visual flare. This might be appealing if you are entertaining.

BOG BLOOD *For 1 serving*

Calories: 109–119

ABV: 4%–5%

INGREDIENTS

one 12 fl. oz. (355 mL) hard seltzer (cranberry flavor)

1.5 fl. oz. (44 mL) cranberry juice

½ oz. (14 g) dried hibiscus flowers

PROCEDURE

Combine the seltzer and the juice. Chop the flower petals and sprinkle into hard seltzer. Stir.

LIME MINT FIZZ *For 1 serving*

Calories: 90–100
ABV: 4%–5%

INGREDIENTS
one 12 fl. oz. (355 mL) hard seltzer (lime flavor)
½ oz. (14 g) fresh mint

PROCEDURE
Bruise the mint leaves and sprinkle into hard seltzer. Stir.

SPICES
You can also add spices, although the best way to do this requires you to pre-pare ahead of time and make a tincture. To do this, put the spice in a small glass jar with a lid. Cover the spice in vodka and let sit in a cool location for at least a few days. For best results, the vodka should cover the spice and leave at least a finger's depth of vodka above. After a week or so, the tincture should be strong enough to use. Use part or all of the spiced vodka for your shot or jigger of alcohol, depending on how strongly the tincture is flavored. This is something you will have to find out for yourself through trial and error.

SPIRITS
Usually, when people think of cocktails they think of a drink made with distilled spirits. Most distilled spirits contain 40% ABV and are labeled 80 proof. These contain 96 calories per fluid ounce (30 mL) or 144 calories per jigger (1.5 fl. oz., or 44 mL) from the alcohol. Other ingredients, if present, may add further calories. Adding one shot (1 fl. oz., or 30 mL) to a standard can (12 fl. oz., 355 mL) of hard seltzer at 5% ABV adds about 3.3% ABV to the beverage, for a total of 8.3% ABV; it also basically doubles the calorie count. Adding a jigger of 80 proof alcohol to a standard can of hard seltzer takes the ABV from 5% to very close to 10%. Such a beverage contains 244 calories—more by volume than a sugary soft drink or most beers, and over twice the calories of the hard seltzer. Of course, you could add less than a shot for a slightly more alcoholic drink, just not one that is 8–10% ABV.

Hard seltzers are not strongly flavored. As such, vodka is a good choice as a mixer in any flavor of hard seltzer because it is not strongly flavored. Some vodka and hard seltzer cocktails may benefit from something to sweeten them. For example, a cranberry hard seltzer mixed with a splash of grapefruit soda and a shot of vodka makes a drink similar to a Sea Breeze. Spirits with strong flavors may work in some mixes, however. For example, gin and lime seltzer go together well. You can also make some sweetish drinks, such as combining orange juice, a peach hard seltzer, and triple sec (an orange liqueur) for a pseudo Fuzzy Navel. You can mix sloe gin with a lemon or lime hard seltzer and a splash of lemon-lime soda for something approximating a Sloe Gin Fizz.

FIZZINESS

If you mix your own hard seltzer, any stirring or agitation that accompanies the mixing will speed the loss of carbon dioxide bubbles. If you are making a single drink, this is not a big deal. However, if you make a larger volume of hard seltzer to serve, perhaps for a party, be aware that it will slowly lose its fizz. The colder you keep the mix, and the less it is agitated, the longer it will retain some spritz. Also, the presence of solids, such as pieces of fresh fruit, will increase the rate of carbonation loss because the solids will serve as nucleation points for CO_2.

Homemade Spiked Seltzers

You can pour seltzer water, flavored or unflavored, into a glass, add a shot of vodka, and voilà—a glass of hard seltzer. If you wanted to be more elaborate, you can combine unflavored seltzer with a shot of vodka and a small amount of flavoring. The flavoring could be fruit juice, soda, or flavor extract. A generic recipe for a hard seltzer might be a jigger of vodka, a splash of juice or soda, and seltzer water, perhaps with a small amount of sugar added.

Before I go on, here is a short chemistry tangent. If 1.0 fl. oz. of 80 proof (40% ABV) vodka was added to seltzer and the total volume of the mixture was 12 fl. oz., the alcohol content would be 3.3% ABV. One jigger (1.5 fl. oz.) of vodka in a total of 12 fl. oz. of seltzer drink would make a 5.0% ABV cocktail. You can also use Everclear (190 proof, 95% ABV) as the liquor. If 1 fl. oz. of 190 proof alcohol is added to seltzer and the total volume of the mixture totals 12 fl. oz. that would be a 7.9% ABV cocktail. In these three examples calculating alcohol by volume, I specified the total volume of the mixture is 12 fl. oz. for a reason. If you poured exactly 11 fl. oz. of seltzer water and exactly 1.0 fl. oz. of vodka into a glass, the volume would be slightly less than 12 fl. oz. In fact, if you mixed 1,000 mL of ethanol with 1,000 mL of water, the total combined volume would only be 1,960 mL, 40 mL less than the 2,000 mL you might expect. If you weighed the water and ethanol separately and then combined them, the mixture would—of course—weigh the same as their combined weights. No part of either liquid has disappeared. The two are just occupying a smaller volume than they did as individual solutions. Some of the total volume "disappears" because some of the ethanol molecules slip into the tiny spaces between water molecules. In the case of mixing a single serving of hard seltzer this phenomenon is barely noticeable. But as the volumes used become larger, the difference adds up.

Mixing your own hard seltzers using seltzer water, spirits, and flavoring can be more economical than buying commercially brewed hard seltzers, which, in the United States at time of writing, generally cost in the neighborhood of $1.20 per 12 fl. oz. serving. A liter of flavored seltzer water generally costs around $0.80, making the price of 12 fl. oz. about $0.30. The price of a liter of vodka—which would yield 33 one-ounce shots or 22 jiggers—varies depending on the brand and local taxes, but would have to exceed $30 per liter (or $22.50 per 750 mL) to make homemade hard seltzer more expensive. If you bought a liter bottle of vodka for $20, which is far from the cheapest available, and you used one shot for every hard seltzer you mixed, your total cost would be $0.90 per 12 fl. oz serving.

Another reason to blend hard seltzer from seltzer water and vodka is that you can use flavorings different from those found in typical hard seltzers. In particular, you can use real fruit juices or fresh-squeezed citrus fruits. This should taste better than the flavorings used in the commercial beverages—and it will also increase the number of different types of flavorings above what is added to commercial hard seltzers. You can also add a bit more and have the beverage more flavorful. This would, however, probably come at the expense of having more sugars in the mix and hence more calories. Of course, the biggest benefit of making your own is that you can make exactly the drink you want. Mango hibiscus lemon limeade? Sure, why not?

APPENDIX A

MAKING HARD SELTZER AT HOME – A PRIMER FOR FIRST TIME FERMENTATIONISTS

SOME FANS OF HARD SELTZER might want to try making their own at home. The best approach, I think, is to learn basic home beer brewing and move from there into brewing hard seltzers. The skills you learn brewing beer at home are transferrable to making seltzers. And making beer at home has a higher probability of success than making hard seltzers with no previous experience. If this is the approach you would like to take, see Appendix B for a crash course on homebrewing.

However, some hard seltzer fans may not have any interest in beer. With this in mind, here is one way to make small, 1.0-gallon (3.8 L) batches of hard seltzer at home, using a minimal amount of specialized equipment. (See table A.1 for a list of equipment you do need.)

As you will gather if you read the rest of this book, the basic process of making a hard seltzer involves fermenting a sugar solution, adding flavors to it, and carbonating the beverage. The first part—fermenting the sugar solution—is the most difficult.

Without specialized equipment, especially an activated carbon filter, you will not be able to make a crystal clear, colorless hard seltzer at home. With some attention to detail, however, you will be able to make a generally clear beverage with just a little color. And if you use natural flavoring, you can call any haze a feature, not a bug.

Table A.1 Basic equipment needed for making hard seltzer

❑ 2.0 gal. (7.6 L) pot
❑ large spoon, to stir sugar solution
❑ 1.0 gal. (3.8 L) glass jug with cap
❑ funnel that fits the jug's opening
❑ balloon (and pin or needle)
❑ 11× 12 fl. oz. (355 mL) beer bottles
or
❑ 5× 25 fl. oz. (750 mL) wine bottles

To begin with, you need to make a sugar solution to ferment. This sugar solution is your *sugar wash*. Your best bet is to use ordinary table sugar (also called cane sugar or sucrose) mixed with a small amount of malt extract. For a 1.0 gal. (3.8 L) batch, 9.0 oz. (260 g) of sugar and 2.0 oz. (57 g) of light or extra light dried malt extract will work well. Malt extract is a product used in home beer brewing. Although malt extract will add a small amount of color to your hard seltzer, it will also contribute nutrients that will help the yeast ferment the mixture efficiently. It is better if your malt extract is the type sold at homebrewing stores, but malt extract for baking can also be used. Dried malt extract will store longer, but liquid malt extract may have a lighter color, providing it is fresh. If you do not have malt extract, 11 oz. (310 g) of sugar will work. This all-sucrose solution will yield a clearer beverage but may take longer to ferment.

This sugar mixture in 1.0 gal. of water will yield 4% alcohol by volume (ABV) when fermented. If you add more sugar the hard seltzer will be higher in alcohol. However, the more sugar you add the more likely your fermentation is to fail. You can try for a 5% ABV beverage, but the odds of failure go up. See table A.2 for possible sugar blends to make hard seltzers between 3.5% and 5.5% ABV.

Table A.2 Percent alcohol by weight (ABV) by weight
of sugar added per 1.0 gal. (3.8 L) of solution

ABV	Weight of sugar
3.5%	10.00 oz. (280 g)
4.0%	11.00 oz. (310 g)
4.5%	12.50 oz. (350 g)
5.0%	14.00 oz. (400 g)
5.5%	15.25 oz. (430 g)

Notes: Sugar addition can be a mixture of roughly 80% table sugar and 20% dried malt extract or 100% sugar.

You should mix the sugar solution in a 2.0-gallon (~8 L) or larger pot. Before adding the water to your sugar, squeeze half a lime into your pot and add 4.0–6.0 fl. oz. (120–180 mL) of fruit juice to flavor the beverage. (Flavors are not added until later in commercial herd seltzer production, but adding the fruit juice now increases your odds of having a successful fermentation.) If using a strongly flavored juice you should add the smaller amount; obviously, for less strongly flavored juice you should add the higher amount. If possible, use a juice that does not contain preservatives. You can squeeze your own if you cannot find a juice of the type of fruit you like.

Add enough water to make a little over 1.0 gal. (3.8 L) of sugar wash and heat it to a boil. (You will lose some water to evaporation.) Once boiling, add 1.5–2.0 tsp. of dried yeast. This can be baker's yeast, even expired baker's yeast. It will serve as nutrients for the active yeast that will be added later. You can also use the type of yeast nutrient sold for home beer brewing and add 1.0–1.5 tsp. per gallon (3.8 L). If you are brewing with just sugar, add 20% more dried yeast or yeast nutrient.

Boil the mixture for 15 minutes. At the end of the boil, turn off the heat, place the lid on the pot, and cool it in a sink of cold water. After 5 minutes, drain the sink and refill it with more cold water. This time, though, add a pound or two of ice. When the outside of the pot is cool to the touch, transfer the solution to a 1.0 gal. (~4 L) jug that has a sealable cap and that has been thoroughly cleaned and sanitized. The jug can be sanitized by filling it with water and adding 1 tablespoon of bleach. Let it sit for 5 minutes, then empty the bleach solution and rinse the jug three times with water. A funnel will help you pour the solution from the pot to the jug.

Put the cap (which should also be sanitized) on the gallon jug and shake it for 2–3 minutes. This will introduce air into the sugar solution, which will help the yeast. Make sure the jug is dry as it is easy to lose your grip on wet glass.

Open the jug again and add yeast. This can be 2 tsp. of (fresh) active dried baker's yeast or, better yet, half a 5 g sachet of wine yeast such as Lalvin's EC-1118 or D-47. Fermentis also makes a dried beer yeast called SafAle US-05 that will work well. Use approximately 2.5 g of either wine or beer yeast. (Wine and beer yeasts come in either 5 g or 11 g packets, and you can just eyeball it. Adding slightly more yeast than is needed will not harm your hard seltzer.)

Take an uninflated balloon and make a pinhole in it. Stretch the neck of the balloon over the opening of the jug. Store the jug, away from light, somewhere at room temperature (or better yet, slightly below). In about a day the yeast will start fermenting the sugar wash and the ballon will inflate. After a week or so, the balloon will deflate, and this will mean the fermentation is almost over. Leave it, with the balloon still in place, for another three days. Instead of a balloon you can also use a drilled stopper and an airlock, which are available at homebrewing shops.

Once fermentation is finished, pour the uncarbonated hard seltzer into a clean, sanitized 2.0 gal. (~4 L) pot. You can sanitize with bleach again. Be sure to rinse the pot thoroughly, though. Add ¼ cup (50 g) of sugar to a smaller pot and dissolve in as little water as you can manage. Heat the solution as you start adding water and it will dissolve faster and into less liquid. Simmer this sugar solution lightly for 5 minutes. Try not to boil so hard that the solution turns yellow. Stir the sugar solution thoroughly into the hard seltzer and transfer it to sealable bottles. Screw-top beer bottles or screw-top wine bottles from beer or wine you have drunk will work. The bottles should be cleaned and sanitized before you fill them. Check to see that the screw tops can be re-secured. Leave a little headspace in each bottle, as much as you would normally see in a commercially produced beer or wine. When transferring the hard seltzer to bottles, try to minimize the amount of splashing. To bottle 1.0 gal. (3.8 L) of hard seltzer, you will need eleven 12 fl. oz. (355 mL) beer bottles or five 25 fl. oz. (750 mL) wine bottles.

Set the bottles somewhere at room temperature or slightly higher. It is best to place them in a box and put the box inside a large (unused) garbage bag in case one of them ruptures. Although rupturing is not very likely, it can happen with thin bottles.

After two weeks, place one bottle in the fridge and let it chill for three days. Then open it and try it. If the hard seltzer is carbonated (and it most likely will be), place the other bottles in the fridge. If not, wait another three days and try it with another bottle.

Homemade hard seltzer will not age and become better. Drink your creation within a month or so of bottling it and start another batch as soon as possible.

The keys to success in making hard seltzer at home are as follows. Clean all your equipment thoroughly. Any surface or object that will contact the sugar wash after it has been cooled should be sanitized. Yeast is a living organism. To ferment the sugar wash adequately, yeast needs nutrients, a little bit of oxygen (dissolved into the sugar wash), and to be held in the proper temperature range. Be sure the sugar wash is cooled to around room temperature before adding the yeast and hold the fermentation at room temperature or slightly below.

APPENDIX B

HOMEBREWING BEER FOR THE FIRST TIME FERMENTATIONIST

Most of the procedures involved in making a hard seltzer will seem familiar to homebrewers and home winemakers. However, if you have never brewed beer or made wine at home, you may have trouble understanding the rationale behind some of the steps. So, here is a review of how beer is made at home. Understanding these procedures will allow you to see that making a hard seltzer can be thought of as just a twist on making beer. And, as a bonus, you will be able to make beer at home too.

Brewing beer and making hard seltzer share some similarities. In both, the maker produces a sugary solution that is then fermented by yeast. In the case of beer, the sugary solution is called *wort* and it is made from malted grains. In both cases, the yeast consumes the sugars and produces alcohol (ethanol), carbon dioxide (CO_2), and heat. The amount of alcohol produced depends on the amount of sugar in solution and the ability of the yeast to consume it.

The more sugar you start with, and the closer the yeast comes to completely consuming it, the more alcohol. In the case of beer, the finished product is a beverage with a relatively low amount of sugar and a (relatively) high amount of ethanol because the yeast has consumed most, but not all, of the sugar. Beer gets its primary flavors from the malted grains and the hops. Some beers may acquire additional flavors through barrel aging, souring, or other processes.

As with beer brewing, hard seltzer production begins by boiling a sugary substance, known as the *wash*, or sugar wash. However, no ingredients that add color or flavor are added during the boil. If fact, throughout the stages of heating and fermenting the wash, the hard seltzer brewer initially attempts to make the beverage as free of color, flavor, and aroma as is possible. The flavor of a hard seltzer is added at the very end of the process.

EQUIPMENT FOR HOMEBREWING

You can begin making beer at home with a relatively small amount of specialized equipment. See table B.1 for a listing of the recommended minimum equipment set required to brew beer. Most home beer brewing and winemaking shops will sell kits that contain all the needed equipment. Many also have "advanced" kits that contain additional useful tools. Homebrewing shops will also sell the necessary ingredients. An equipment kit designed for brewing beer at home will also allow you to make hard seltzers.

Food-grade buckets and glass (or plastic) carboys are often used by beginning homebrewers as vessels for fermenting. Intermediate or advanced homebrewers may invest in stainless steel fermentors.

One aspect important to brewing is cleanliness. Wort can support the growth of many different types of microorganisms, whether yeasts, molds, or bacteria. However, the only "bug" that brewers want growing in their fermentors is yeast. As such, brewers need spotlessly clean and sanitized equipment.

Table B.1 Homebrewing Equipment

Here is a list of equipment that will allow you to brew both hard seltzers and malt extract-based beers in 5.0-gallon (19 L) batches at home. Most homebrew shops sell everything you need as a set. Sometimes the brewpot is sold separately. You may also have many of these items at home or items that can be repurposed for these uses.

Brewpot	Preferably stainless steel and with a volume of at least 5.0 gallons (19 L). A spigot is a nice option
Nylon (or muslin) steeping bags	A large bag capable of loosely containing up to 4.0 lb. (1.8 kg) of crushed grains and a smaller bag capable of holding up to 4.0 oz. (110 g) of pellet hops will allow you to brew almost any homebrew recipe
Long-handled spoon	Preferably stainless steel, but plastic or wood will work. For stirring the wort as it boils
Wort chiller	A simple immersion chiller—made from a coil of copper tubing—is all you need. More complex chillers, such as counterflow or plate chillers are also available
Fermentor	Preferably two; a 7.0-gallon (27 L) food-grade bucket for primary fermentation and a 5.0-gallon (19 L) glass or plastic carboy for conditioning make a nice combo. A spigot on the bucket (and the plastic fermentor) is a nice option
Airlock and stoppers	The stoppers should be drilled to accept the airlocks and sized to fit the bucket and the carboy.
Transfer aids	Depending on whether your vessels have spigots or not, these will include Tygon tubing, a racking cane, an auto-siphon, or some combination of these. Spigoted vessels can be emptied with tubing that fits the spigot. Vessels without a spigot will require a racking cane or auto-siphon.
Hydrometer and test jar	Hydrometers come in multiple ranges; the most common type covers the whole range needed for homebrewing. Smaller range hydrometers can be nice for taking the specific gravity of finished beers.
Thermometer	It helps if it is waterproof
Bottles, caps, and a capper	You will need enough bottles to contain 5.0 gallons (19 L) of beer. This is 53× 12 fl. oz. (355 mL) bottles or 29× 22 fl. oz. (650 mL) bottles
Campden tablets	For treating municipal water sources that contain chlorine compounds
pH meter (optional)	Can come in handy, especially for advanced homebrewers

HOMEBREWING BEER: THE BASICS

The simplest way to brew beer is to make wort from malt extract. This is also the brewing method that is most similar to brewing hard seltzers.

MALT EXTRACT IS CONDENSED WORT

Malt extract is a form of condensed wort. Wort is the sugary solution mentioned earlier—it can be thought of as unfermented beer— and it is typically made from barley malt and hops. Sometimes other unmalted grains, especially corn or rice, are used. Malted barley is barley seed that has been sprouted, dried, and kilned (or sometimes roasted) in an oven. Sprouting and drying takes the hard seed and makes it soft. Kilning "toasts" the husk of the grain a bit and makes it flavorful. Other grains, most notably wheat, may be malted and used in brewing.

Wort contains a lot of sugar, especially the sugar maltose. It also contains a small amount of protein. And, of course, these solids are dissolved in water, which is the most abundant component of wort by weight. Molecules called *alpha acids*, which are derived from hops, give wort its bitterness, but are only present in small quantities.

MALT EXTRACT-BASED BEER

Malt extract-based beer is typically made by dissolving malt extract in water to reconstitute the wort. The wort is typically flavored with steeped specialty grains, which add color as well as flavor. The wort is then boiled. Hops are added during the boil and this imparts bitterness to the beer. The bitterness is intended to balance any sweetness in the beer. After the boil, the wort is cooled and transferred to a fermentor. Air is introduced into the wort and the brewer adds ("pitches") his or her yeast. The yeast consumes the sugars in the wort, transforming the wort into beer. Homebrewed beer is usually packaged in bottles or kegs. For an ale, the whole process takes about two weeks. It takes a few hours to boil and cool the wort, transfer it to a fermentor, and pitch the yeast. It takes only an hour or two to bottle a homebrew-scale batch of beer, and less to keg it.

A typical brewing session for a beer made with malt extract proceeds as explained in the next section. For the nitty gritty details, see the example recipe at the end after reading the general description of the process.

HOMEBREWING BEER WITH MALT EXTRACT: STEP BY STEP

The most important part of brewing is the least glamorous. In order for beer to be free of unpleasant aromas or flavors, all the equipment used in the brewing process must be spotlessly clean. Anything that touches the wort must additionally be sanitized. (Note that cleaning and sanitizing are two different things.) Most homebrew stores sell special cleaners for homebrew equipment. These clean without leaving a residue of detergent on the surfaces they touch. Liquid sanitizers are used to sanitize clean surfaces. Homebrewers typically use either iodine-based sanitizers or acid-based sanitizers. Bleach may be used, but equipment sanitized in bleach must be rinsed thoroughly.

To begin the brew day, the brewer adds water to his or her brewpot. Most homebrewed beer in the US is made in 5.0-gallon (19 L) batches. In this case, the brewer typically adds between 2.5 and 3.5 gallons (9.5–13 L) of water to their 5–7-gallon (19–27 L) brewpot. For an extract-based beer, water with few dissolved minerals works best. The malt extract will contain any required minerals in the brewing process or during fermentation. It is possible to use distilled water. However, almost any municipal water will also work. For the best results, municipal water should be either filtered through activated carbon or treated by adding one Campden tablet per 20 gallons (76 L), or less, of water. Either method will remove chlorine compounds from the water.

The water in the brewpot is heated and some or all of the malt extract is dissolved in the hot water. Withholding a portion of the malt extract until the very end of the boil (the next step) allows for lighter-colored beers to be made. Before the malt extract is dissolved, specialty grains—typically contained in a nylon or muslin bag—are steeped in the hot water. Specialty grains add color and flavor to the wort and subsequent beer. The grains should be crushed and often this is done at the homebrew shop. The steeping bag containing the crushed grains is immersed in the water long enough to extract the colors and flavors required, usually 15–60 minutes. The temperature the specialty grains are steeped at is frequently 150–170°F (66–77°C), although almost any temperature short of boiling will work. After this steeping period, the bag is removed and set aside.

In some cases, the brewer may actually be performing a *mash* when steeping his or her grains. In these cases, the temperature needs to be held between 150°F and 162°F (66–72°C). When mashing, the amount of water used should be just enough to make the consistency of a thin porridge of the crushed grains. (The recipe should specify how to handle the grains.)

Next, after the malt extract has been added to the "grain tea" produced by steeping the grains, the wort is usually boiled for 60 minutes, although times can vary. Near the beginning of the boil, some hops are added. These are called the bittering hops and they confer a level of bitterness to the wort. The heat of the boiling wort serves to extract alpha acids from the hops. It also isomerizes—changes the molecular conformation of—these alpha acids into iso-alpha acids, which are intensely bitter compounds. Most of the bitterness in beer comes from iso-alpha acids. The amount of bitterness the hops confer depends on how long they are boiled and their "strength," given as the percentage of alpha acids in the hops by dried weight. Longer boils and higher alpha acid levels in the hops create more bitter beers. Less bitter beers are usually made by boiling low-alpha acid hops, not by boiling the hops for a shorter period of time. Hops may also be added at other times during the boil. Hops added near to or at the end of the boil impart the aroma of hops to the beer. The aromatic compounds, which are hop oils, responsible for hop aroma are mostly boiled away from the early hop additions.

Near the end of the boil, a *fining* agent called Irish moss (or a preparation of it called Whirlfloc) may be added. This fining agent will settle out and remove some potential haze-causing molecules from the wort. Yeast nutrients may also be added near the end of the boil, although they are not needed for every beer. And of course, if any of the malt extract was withheld earlier, it is added at the very end of the boil.

Boiling sanitizes the wort and is required to extract bittering compounds from the hops. During the boil, solids, called *hot break*, form. The particles of hot break in hot wort look a bit like snowflakes. After boiling, the wort must be cooled to a temperature that will allow the yeast to survive and ferment the solution. Wort chilling can be done by placing the brewpot (with its cover on) in a cold water bath. A sink or bathtub will do for this. Alternatively, a piece of equipment called a wort chiller may be employed. The simplest wort chillers are coils of copper tubing. These are submerged in the wort near the end of the boil to sanitize them. After the boil, cool water is run through the coil to bring down the temperature of the wort. More elaborate chillers move the hot wort through a tube (or through a series of chambers) while cool water moves past it in the opposite direction. These types of wort chiller—either counterflow chillers or plate chillers—additionally transfer the wort to the fermentor.

When the wort is cooled with an immersion chiller, some solid material, called *cold break*, forms and falls to the bottom of the brewpot. When the wort is transferred to the fermentor this cold break is left behind along with the hot break and hop debris. When a counterflow or plate chiller is used, the cold break forms inside the chiller and ends up in the fermentor while the hot break is left behind in the brewpot. The brewer may *rack* (transfer) the beer away from the cold break material before fermentation starts.

After the wort is chilled it must be transferred to the fermentor. (In the case of a counterflow-type chiller, of course, cooling and moving the wort to the fermentor occurs in a single step.) This can be done with a food-grade pump, but most homebrewers simply start a siphon and rely on gravity to move the liquid. The brewpot must be positioned above the fermentor for this to work. Siphoning the liquid can be relatively easy with a piece of equipment called a racking cane, which is a rigid tube attached to some flexible vinyl tubing. The tube goes to the bottom of the brewpot and the tubing leads to the fermentor. The siphon can be "suck started," or the racking cane may be filled with water. Placing the tip of the rigid tube below the surface of the wort and lowering the end of the vinyl tubing will get the siphon started. Alternatively, some brew-pots have a spigot near the bottom. Brewers can attach some vinyl tubing to the spigot and start transferring wort simply by opening the spigot valve.

Once in the fermentor, the wort must be aerated. The yeast will perform much better if there is dissolved oxygen in the wort. Aeration can be performed by simply shaking the fermentor vigorously, or you can "whip" the wort with a large whisk. However, you need to keep this up for about 5 minutes to be effective. Many homebrewers use a sintered aeration stone to inject air or oxygen into their wort. The aeration stone is connected, via nylon tubing, to either an aquarium pump or a small oxygen tank. The gas flows through a HEPA filter on its way to the stone. (Homebrew shops sell the kits for this. Little oxygen tanks are available in the welding section of hardware stores. Medical supply stores may have larger tanks.) Some homebrewers place their aeration stone at the outlet of a counterflow or plate chiller so chilled wort is aerated as it flows into the fermentor.

At this point, it is worthwhile to remember that any surface that touches wort—and especially chilled wort—needs to be sanitized. The heat of the boil will sanitize the brewpot. However, wort chillers need to be sanitized. In the case of an immersion chiller, the (cleaned) chiller is typically placed in the brewpot for the final 5 minutes of boil to allow the heat of the boil to sanitize the chiller. A counterflow-type chiller may be sanitized by running sanitizing solution through it. It must be clean inside for this to work. To clean a counterflow-type chiller, hot cleaning solution may be recirculated though it. The racking cane, if used, must be sanitized also, and do not forget that the inside of the fermentor additionally needs to be sanitized. This is often done by adding some sanitizing solution to the (clean) vessel and swirling it around until the solution wets all of the interior surface. Some sanitizing solutions do not need to be rinsed. In that case, they are simply drained from the vessel before the chilled wort is transferred to them.

Once the wort is boiled, chilled, and aerated, the yeast is added (pitched). In many cases, brewers will make a yeast starter one to three days before brewing their main batch. A yeast starter is a small batch of low-sugar wort intended to raise the proper amount of yeast for the main batch. (The *specific gravity* is a measure of how much sugar is in a wort, with a higher gravity meaning more sugar.) The larger the batch of the beer and the more sugar that is in it, the more yeast is required. Shortly after the yeast is added, fermentation begins.

After the yeast is pitched, the fermentor should be placed somewhere at or slightly below the recommended fermentation temperature, often 60–72°F (16–22°C) for ales and 50–55°F (10–13°C) for lagers. The fermentor is then sealed except for an airlock, or fermentation lock, which allows gases to escape the vessel. Fermentation can take a few days to a few weeks, depending on the fermentation temperature and the amount and type of yeast pitched. A low-gravity ale, such as a mild ale or bitter, may ferment in just three days. A medium or high-gravity lager, such as a *bockbier*, will often take a couple of weeks or more. Strong beers—high-gravity beers with a lot of sugar in their wort—can take up to a couple of months to finish. During fermentation, the CO_2 produced by the yeast will cause the airlock to bubble. The amount of bubbles produced is a rough gauge to the vigor of the fermentation, provided the fermentor is otherwise sealed.

After fermentation finishes, ales will typically clear in a few days when held at their fermentation temperature. A layer of yeast and other materials, collectively called *trub*, will cover the bottom of the fermentor. In some cases, an ale may be cold-conditioned for a few days. Lagers require a conditioning period after primary fermentation. The conditioning process is called *lagering* and allows any yeast still in suspension to clean up the "green beer" flavors. Generally, the temperature of the beer is dropped to near freezing and held for a while until sampling indicates the beer is "clean." In particular, a clean beer should be free of a buttery or butterscotch-like flavor due to the presence of a yeast by-product called diacetyl.

Most of the time, properly brewed beer will fall clear on its own. This is especially true if the beer is stored cold for few days before serving. Commercial brewers filter their beer to obtain crystal clarity. Most homebrewers will either enjoy their reasonably clear beer, or use fining to further clarify it. Gelatin or isinglass (a preparation made from the swim bladders of fish) work well to clear any residual yeast in solution. The Irish moss added in the boil should have removed at least most of the proteins present in the wort that are responsible for haze in the final beer. Polyvinylpolypyrrolidone (PVPP) is often used to remove tannins, which also contribute to beer haze. Fining agents work by stirring a thick solution of the fining agent into the beer and letting it settle out. The beer can then be racked away from the sediment containing the fining agent and the material it has removed.

Once the beer is fermented, conditioned, and clarified, it is ready to be packaged. Homebrewed beer is usually either bottled or kegged. Canning requires equipment that is prohibitively expensive at the individual homebrew scale.

For bottling, the beer can be transferred away from the trub to a bottling bucket. The brewer adds a small amount of sugar and the beer is transferred again, this time into bottles. Unfiltered beer, even clear beer, has some yeast cells remaining in suspension. In the bottle, the yeast will ferment the added sugar, producing ethanol and CO_2. The amount of ethanol produced is slight, but the amount of CO_2 produced is enough to give the beer its required fizz in a sealed bottle.

Homebrewed beer can also be kegged and stored under CO_2 pressure. The CO_2 will, over the course of several days, dissolve into the beer and carbonate it. Cornelius kegs, the type that used to be used for dispensing soda pop, are the most widely used type of keg in homebrewing.

Homebrewing is an interesting hobby and also teaches many of the skills needed for mead making and winemaking. And, of course, brewing beer at home is very similar to producing hard seltzers at home. The biggest key to success with homebrewing is keeping your equipment spotlessly clean and sanitizing any surface that will contact chilled wort or beer. The second biggest key to success is running an ordered fermentation. This involves pitching an adequate amount of yeast, ensuring proper yeast nutrition (mostly through proper aeration), and holding the fermentation at a steady temperature in the correct temperature range for the yeast.

Homebrewing need not be daunting. Now you are armed with knowledge of the basics, you can try your hand at brewing the American pale ale recipe below. Good luck and happy brewing!

MALT EXTRACT HOMEBREW RECIPE

PATRICK HENRY PALE ALE *To make 5.0 gal. (19 L)*

American-style Pale Ale

Original (starting) gravity: 1.052
Final gravity: 1.011
ABV: 5.3%
Bitterness: 40 IBU (international bittering units)
Color: 11 SRM (corresponds to a pale-to-medium amber)

INGREDIENTS

Malt extract and specialty grains
4.25 lb. (1.93 kg) light dried malt extract
1.3 lb. (590 g) US 2-row pale malt
8.0 oz. (230 g) crystal malt (40°L)
3.0 oz. (85 g) crystal malt (60°L)

Hops

0.38 oz. (11 g)	Simcoe (13% alpha acids, or AA), boiled for 60 minutes (13 IBU)
0.50 oz. (14 g)	Centennial (10% AA), boiled for 30 minutes (14 IBU)
0.63 oz. (18 g)	Cascade (7% AA), boiled for 15 minutes (9 IBU)
0.25 oz. (7 g)	Amarillo (8% AA), boiled for 15 minutes (4 IBU)
0.63 oz. (18 g)	Cascade (7% AA), boiled for 0 minutes (0 IBUs)
0.25 oz. (7 g)	Amarillo (8% AA), boiled for 0 minutes (0 IBUs)
0.75 oz. (21 g)	Cascade dry hops, added in secondary fermentor
0.50 oz. (14 g)	Amarillo dry hops, added in secondary fermentor

Other additions
1 tsp. Irish moss, boiled for 15 minutes
¼ tsp. yeast nutrients, boiled for 15 minutes

Yeast

Wyeast 1056 American Ale (liquid yeast), White Labs WLP001 California Ale (liquid yeast), or Fermentis US-05 (dried yeast)

Use a 1.5 qt. (1.4 L) yeast starter for liquid yeasts

Additions at bottling

5.0 oz. (140 g) corn sugar, to prime bottles for 2.6 volumes of CO_2

PROCEDURE

Crush the grains (either at the homebrew shop or your home, if you have a grain mill). Place the crushed grains in a steeping bag. In your brewpot, steep the crushed grains in 3.0 qt. (2.8 L) of water at 152°F (67°C) for 45 minutes. Remove grains and add water to the pot to make 3.5 gal. (13 L) of wort. Add roughly half of the malt extract and bring the wort to a boil.

Boil the wort for 60 minutes, adding hops, Irish moss, and yeast nutrients at times indicated. Stir in remaining malt extract during final 10 minutes of the boil. Chill the wort to 68 °F (20 °C) and transfer to your fermentor, leaving any sediment behind. Top up to 5.0 gal. (19 L) with cool water. (This volume does not account for the small amount of beer that will be lost in the fermentor due to sediment.)

Pitch the yeast after topping off to 5 gal. Ferment at 68°F (20°C). After fermentation stops, let beer settle for two to three days, then rack to secondary fermentor—leaving any trub behind—and add the dry hops (preferably bagged in a nylon bag). For best results, dry hop in a carboy with as little headspace as possible. Dry hop for five to six days, then rack to keg or bottling bucket, for a yield of 5.0 gal. (19 L) minus any losses from leaving the trub and wet hops behind. Dissolve priming sugar and then add to the bottling bucket. Transfer to bottles and store warm for two weeks to allow beer to carbonate to 2.6 volumes of CO_2.

INDEX